HAUNTED
BODMIN MOOR

Jason Higgs

The
History
Press

I would like to dedicate this book to my parents, Pamela and Gordon Higgs, whose rational beliefs and continued support have enabled me to question all my paranormal experiences and allowed me to pursue a logical and natural answer for those events that may at first appear supernatural.

First published 2012

The History Press
The Mill, Brimscombe Port
Stroud, Gloucestershire, GL5 2QG
www.thehistorypress.co.uk

British Library Cataloguing in Publication Data.
A catalogue record for this book is available from the British Library.

ISBN 978 0 7524 6332 2
Typesetting and origination by The History Press

Contents

Foreword

My interest in the paranormal never came from a personal experience, unlike other people's curiosity for the unknown. Mine was borne out of a passion for all things science fiction and the possibility that fictional science could be bordering on fact. I was born and raised in the UK but now live with my family in America. After many years investigating the supernatural, I became the 'technology guy' on the smash hit Sy-Fy channel series 'Ghost Hunters International', investigating the unknown around the world. During my travels I have had the opportunity to capture some amazing exotic locations on camera and in 2009 I released my first publication of photography, entitled *Wish You Were Here*. It is obvious that Jason also has an appetite for photography and *Haunted Bodmin Moor* contains some moody and intriguing images from his travels around the Cornish countryside.

From communications with Jason, I've discovered that Bodmin Moor is more than just an interest for him — it is a passion. From growing up on the moor, sharing his day-to-day life with his parents, to hair-raising paranormal experiences within his family home, Jason's accounts are effectively put into print.

Historically, Bodmin Moor, which was first farmed 4,000 years ago, has much of its history remaining within its soil. Prehistoric and medieval artefacts lay untouched and unspoiled until this day.

The vastness of the moor has always invoked both fear and awe to its locals and those weary travellers who are simply passing through. However, its beauty and its legends blended into one, as the stories were passed down from generation to generation, inspiring artists and writers alike to create wondrous pieces of work.

So, please sit back and learn about another side to the astounding moor, from someone who has lived and breathed it their whole life.

Paul Bradford
Ghost Hunters International, 2012

Acknowledgements

I would like to take this opportunity to thank a number of exceptional friends and family who have guided me along the correct path whilst writing this book. I would like to say a special thank you to my colleagues at Supernatural Investigations: Kevin Hynes, who authored *Haunted Plymouth*, and Stuart Andrews, who co-authored our first book, *Paranormal Cornwall*. Also special thanks to Clare Buckland and Becky Andrews, who have contributed to many investigations over the years.

Also thanks go to Paul Bradford, Technical Manager for Ghost Hunters International, for his kind words, time and effort in writing the foreword to this book.

Finally, I would like to acknowledge all those that provided the kind of information you would not find in a book or online, those that live and breathe the moor and have done so for many years.

Every effort has been made to trace copyright holders and to obtain their permission for the use of copyright material. I apologise to anyone who may have been inadvertently missed out and will gladly receive any information enabling me to rectify any error or omission in subsequent editions.

Introduction

AS I write this, I am sitting atop a granite anomaly on top of the Cheesewring on the edge of Bodmin Moor. It is a warm sunny day in April and the horizon is so clear I can see for miles and miles. To the east I can just make out the city of Plymouth, across the border in Devon. To the west the view stretches out over the rest of Bodmin Moor, enveloping the A30, one of the two main roads into Cornwall. This arterial route through the county passes some of the most well-known haunted locations in this desolate landscape, including such locations as Jamaica Inn, an eighteenth-century coaching inn which still lines the old route from Bodmin to Launceston, an area popularised by the 1936 publication

The author sitting on a rock formation at the top of Stowes Hill.

View of Rough Tor from the car park.

of Daphne du Mauriers' aptly named novel, *Jamaica Inn*. Also mentioned in this book is the disreputable vicar of Altarnun, a village situated just a few miles up the A30 towards Okehampton. Further west, past the A30 and deep in the heart of the moor, lies Davidstow and Rough Tor, where the heinous murder of Charlotte Dymond was committed in 1844. To the north, Sharp Tor can be seen. A blip on the landscape that from my current position looks small and easy to climb, yet once you reach the foot of the tor, you realise how steep and daunting the rocky nubbin is. Apart from the sound of the odd motorbike, it is hard to imagine that I am living in the twenty-first century. The moor is vast and baron, littered with mined granite and windswept trees. A lonely wild pony wanders past and stops to chomp on any edible tufts of grass, while white dots of sheep can be seen bobbing along between ancient stone boundaries.

As you take time to process the view you realise that the moorland is hiding centuries of history in plain sight. In the distance, on Stowes Hill, you can see the mathematical placement of standing stones called the Hurlers, a Bronze-Age stone temple consisting of three large stone circles. The name derives from a legend that men and women were playing Cornish hurling on a Sunday and were mystically turned to stone as a punishment.

From ancient battles fought hard with swords and gauntlets, and lost and weary travellers, perishing in the hidden bogs the moor has to offer, to ruinous engine houses, which once furiously mined the granite beneath for copper and tin, now dotted across the moorland, it is not hard to understand why this moor has so many of its own myths, legends and ghost stories.

Bodmin Moor is not for the faint-hearted and you soon realise that you should approach this place with intrepid caution.

Jason Higgs, 2012
www.supernaturalinvestigations.org.uk

1

A Brief History of Bodmin Moor

BODMIN Moor is a wild and untamed expanse of granite moorland situated in the north-east of Cornwall. It covers approximately 80 square miles and its recorded history dates back to 10,000 BC. It is believed that hunter-gatherers wandered the moorland, at that time thick with trees and shrubs, searching for wildebeests or deer from which to make lunch for their secluded communities. Following on from this period the woodland was eventually cleared and the land became arable for farming. During this time, about 4500 BC, various megalithic monuments were erected; mainly cairns and stone circles for use as ceremonial sites. The unusual natural compilation of stones, such as the Cheesewring on Stowes Hill, would have been viewed in the same way. As time passed into the birth of the Bronze Age the creation of the structures continued, and it is believed that over 300 further cairns and stone circles were created.

More than 200 settlements have been recorded and found on the moor, with various granite walls and barrows littering the land. Various flint work has been discovered by archaeologists on the moor, suggesting that the hunter gatherers were skilful in the art of flint knapping, which is the process of shaping the flint piece into a sharp useful hunting tool. In 2005, Channel 4's *Time Team* travelled to Bodmin Moor to investigate what historical secrets the sweeping landscape may be hiding. They particularly focussed on two specific sites at the base of Rough Tor. The first was a 500-metre long stone cairn, running on an east–west alignment pointing towards the tor. The second was a concentration of circular structures, thought to be Bronze-Age roundhouses, and other features indicating a Bronze-Age village. The find confirmed that there was indeed evidence of a Bronze-Age village, with discovery of pottery dating from about 1500 BC. They also

View from the top of Stowes Hill with the Cheesewring stone formation on the left.

King Arthur's Hall at Garrow Tor. (Photo courtesy of Simon Lewis, www.westcountryviews.co.uk)

Dozmary Pool in the height of winter. It looks like it could go on for miles.

found evidence for complex construction in the cairn, with retaining walls and a rubble infill in the middle. While no specific date was found for this structure, it is believed it ranged from the Neolithic period. Over time the moorland population grew and farming became rife, with many farm structures being erected. Today, there are around 500 farm holdings with about 10,000 cows, 55,000 sheep and 1,000 horses and ponies.

The moor has some surprising mystical connections: although it is difficult to prove the existence of King Arthur or his link to Bodmin Moor, the landscape itself boasts a number of areas named after the legendary king himself. Legend has it that King Arthur, or Arthur Pendragon, was the leader of Britain in the late fifth and early sixth centuries –

leading the defence of Britain against the Saxons in the early sixth century. Whether or not the legend of King Arthur is true, it is known that various hotspots around Bodmin Moor are littered with Arthurian remnants, such as King Arthur's Castle, which can be found near Bodmin Moor at Tintagel. With regard to the moor itself, three locations give rise to the name of King Arthur; the first is a man-shaped depression in granite near Trewortha Tor, known locally as Arthurs Bed. Legend has it that this is the place that Arthur laid his head during his travels. The second location is known as King Arthur's Hall and is a prehistoric stone-lined enclosure. An ancient wall of stone surrounds a soggy marshland area that looks like the dilapidated remains of a hall. The whole area

Remnants of old engine houses line the horizon in the Gonamena Valley.

is known as King Arthur's Downs and is located near Garrow Tor.

Finally, and probably the most well-known connection, is Dozmary Pool near Coliford Lake. As the tale is told, the 'Lady of the Lake', the holder of the mighty sword Excalibur, lived beneath the rippling waters of Dozmary Pool. It is believed that King Arthur rowed out to the middle of the lake, where the sword mysteriously rose from beneath. After months of fierce battles with the mystical sword, Sir Bedivere and Arthur returned to the pool to give back the sword to the Lady of the Lake. As Arthur lay bleeding and dying after the Battle of Camlann, Sir Bedivere threw the sword as hard as he could into the air before a hand rose from the pool and grasped the airborne weapon. Slowly, the hand withdrew into the water and the sword and lady were never seen again.

Dozmary Pool has another mysterious connection with regards to an early seventeenth-century magistrate known as Jan Tregeagle. Tregeagle had a harsh and particularly evil reputation. Over time certain stories arose about the magistrate that indicated that he had murdered his wife and made a pact with the Devil. It was alleged that, whilst searching for deviant exploits, he made a Faustian bargain with the Devil and was blessed with riches and power beyond comprehension. However, on death, he was damned to the bottomless pits of Dozmary Pool. It has been proven in recent years that the lake is not bottomless; however, people who visit the lake have reported hearing unusual moans and groans around the lake which have been attributed to the spirit or ghost of the magistrate himself.

The moor has been romanticised on occasion over the years and has played many parts in novels, dramas and tales of the sea. The moor is home to some amazing inns which will be covered in more detail later, but an example would be the splendour of Jamaica Inn, near Bolventor. A hotel/pub steeped in history and known around the world due to its portrayal in Daphne du Maurier's bestselling novel *Jamaica Inn*. This tale of love and betrayal was later immortalised in a film of the same name in 1939, directed by the well-known suspense director of the mid-twentieth century, Alfred Hitchcock. The film and book brought Cornwall and Bodmin Moor its own fame and people travelled from all over the world to visit the moor and, in particular, Jamaica Inn. Of course, the inn is still standing today and has managed to generate its own fame as a place of eerie happenings. Far from du Maurier's romantic portrayal, Jamaica Inn hides a sinister past with a tremendous amount of people experiencing paranormal activity here.

A short distance from Bolventor is Rough Tor and Brown Willy. Simply mentioning Rough Tor conjures up a popular name among the locals; Charlotte Dymond, the ill-fated eighteen-year-old who was cut down in the prime of youth by a murderous lover.

With the advance of the copper and tin mining era in the eighteenth century, the moor was ripped apart as granite was churned out and large open mineshafts were dug deep into the land. The con-struction of a railway to ship the mined elements to nearby Liskeard, known as the Caradon Railway, was built alongside Caradon Hill and continued up to the Cheesewring. With such large construction and mining there was inevitably a large workforce from nearby villages. Many people at that time worked long hours and did not have the luxury of vehicles to transport them from their home to their place of work. Many workers would be up at 4 a.m., walk 5 miles or more to the mines before working a twelve-hour day and then walking the same 5 miles home. The next day would be the same, probably for seven days a week.

One such stonecutter chose not to travel and decided to live on the moor itself. At this time the village of Minions would not have existed, so living on the moor would have been a very bleak place. Daniel Gumb was born in Linkinhorne in 1703 and, shortly after getting married, moved to the base of Stowes Hill at the Cheesewring – now Cheesewring quarry. As you can imagine, at that time there were no houses or huts to live in, so Daniel constructed his own house from slabs of granite and by digging deep into the moor. Using a slab of granite 30ft by 10ft as a roof, Daniel managed to use other granite slabs as supports to finally construct a three-roomed house with a chimney. Imagining that this was a pretty basic and bleak place to live, high on the moor, with the winter wind howling and the cold of the granite, it is hard to believe that Daniel raised nine children here.

The relocated Daniel Gumb's Cave at the base of Stowes Hill.

The Trippet Stones near St Breward.

Daniel married a total of three times while living on the moor. One stone erection bears the inscription 'D GUMB 1735', which is believed to be the date of his third marriage. If this story is not strange enough, Daniel was a keen mathematician, astronomer and philosopher, mostly self-taught. He used to sit on his roof gazing up at the stars, night after night, and, when not working, was partial to solving mathematical problems by day. On his roof he carved Euclid's Theorem – the same theorem can be found carved on other slabs of granite near the disused railway! Daniel eventually died in 1773, after most of his offspring had moved to the Americas. Unfortunately, due to the excavation of the quarry, Daniel's house was moved from its original location but can still be found on the moor near the base of the Cheesewring. Only the roof and inscribed doorpost remains from the original construction, but it still gives you an idea of what his humble abode would have looked like.

The vast landscape of Bodmin Moor has been home to many mystical and paranormal events over the centuries. From Pagan and Druid rituals to reports of UFOs and big cat sightings, the moor is a place that is certainly not short of a story or two. In this book I hope to take you on a journey of Bodmin Moor by telling you some of the most poignant ghost stories that exist about this prehistoric landscape. So, please sit comfortably and let this book unravel the mysteries of Bodmin Moor.

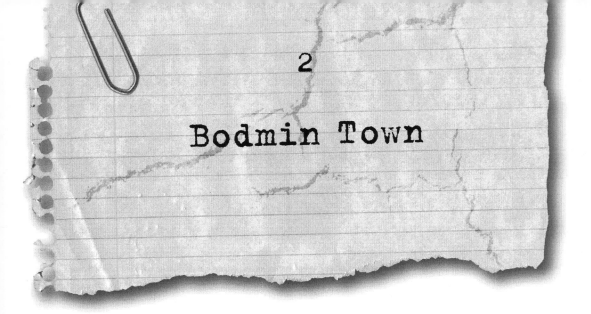

2

Bodmin Town

ALTHOUGH not directly located on the moor itself, the barren landscape was named after the old town. This is probably due to Bodmin being the oldest market town in Cornwall, being mentioned in the Domesday Book of 1066. The name Bodmin is believed to mean 'House of Monks' and this is easy to understand, as St Petroc moved a monastery from Padstow to the town in the tenth century. This was the religious centre of Bodmin for many centuries until Henry VIII closed the priory in 1538. Bodmin itself is steeped in history and has seen three different types of monks over time. The original monastery was converted to an Augustinian Priory in the twelfth century and, following this, it saw the introduction of Franciscan Friars in the thirteenth century. In 1349, Bodmin was hit by the Black Death, which all but wiped out the population at that time. Today, Bodmin is a flourishing town with over 12,000 people (as of the 2001 census), which has seen the town recover from the harsh times fraught with three separate Cornish Rebellions, all of which failed. Notably, Bodmin is renowned for a building of 1779 that is now reported to be one of the most haunted locations in Britain. It is, of course, Bodmin Jail.

Bodmin Jail

I first wrote about Bodmin Jail in 2009 with my co-author Stuart Andrews in *Paranormal Cornwall*, after spending an evening investigating this wondrous building. The jail has seen many different faces, young and old, pass through its doors while it was a prison. Unlike today's prisons, with rooms kitted out with televisions and computers, and public areas with pool tables and gyms, life in an eighteenth-century prison was a whole other existence. If you were lucky, then your time inside would have been disease-free and eventually you may leave the lock-up alive. Along the way you would have been subjected to gruesome conditions, such as scouring the floor looking for scraps of food. Windowless openings meant that the harsh winter storms would transform the cells into freezing pits of despair. During the day you would have been exposed to endless hours performing repugnant tasks supervised by guards who may subject you to outrageous beatings. Your incarceration would probably have been for what we class today as minor offences, such as sheep rustling or stealing apples from a neighbouring vineyard. Children were treated no differently to adults and many were locked up in the foreboding building for stealing food because they and their families were starving.

Overcrowding was common within the jail and overcapacity within a single cell meant that many people died as a result of asphyxiation or being crushed. Others contracted illnesses or pneumonia and without proper treatment died as a result. Prison deaths were significantly lower than deaths attributed to sentencing. In the 1770s, 241 offences were punishable by hanging. Between 1785 and 1820 these included burglary, robbery with violence, sheep stealing, highway robbery, killing animals and arson. Only twelve out of the thirty-six hangings were for murder. From 1821 to 1909 there were a total of seventeen hangings. Thirteen of these were for murder, with

Front elevation of the Naval wing at Bodmin Jail.

the others accredited to arson, highway robbery, house-breaking and bestiality. There were a total of fifty-six hangings at Bodmin between 1785 and 1909.

One of the most notorious executions at Bodmin Jail was that of Matthew Weekes (*see* chapter three), convicted of murdering Charlotte Dymond. Due to media coverage of this case, his hanging brought many thousands of people to witness his ultimate demise. Regardless of whether Matthew was guilty or not, many people claim to have seen his spirit at the jail. Is it his ghost protesting his innocence, or could he be seeking forgiveness by finally admitting his role in the murder of such a young, innocent and beautiful maid servant? Matthew has never left the grounds of Bodmin Jail, as his body is reported to be buried under the old coal yard.

Another well-known story from the vaults of the prison is the tale of the Lightfoot brothers, a pair of highwaymen who eluded justice for quite a while. William and James Lightfoot laid in wait for a wealthy miller called Nevell Norway. The Lightfoot brothers knew his regular route from work to home and, on one occasion, when Nevell trotted passed them on his horse, they took the opportunity to rob him, knocking him off his horse before clubbing him to death. Forensic skills and face recognition were not available in the 1840s and for a while it seemed the perpetrators would go unpunished. This was until a top detective from London was called to assist in the case and after a reward was put forward for information, the Lightfoot brothers were caught. After a few days in custody the brothers finally admitted to the murder and both were hanged at Bodmin Jail. Over £3,000 was raised in total for Nevell's widow and six children – a large amount back then, which goes to show the sympathy shown by the public.

Women were treated no differently at the jail and two examples are Elizabeth

The coalyard at the back of Bodmin Jail, where Matthew Weekes is believed to be buried.

Cummins and Selina Wadge, who were hanged in 1828 and 1878 respectively. Elizabeth's ghost is said to wander the dark corridors of the jail and it has been said that visitors have heard a woman crying over her baby, which is believed to be twenty-two-year-old Elizabeth, who was hanged for the murder of her son.

One evening, after giving birth out of wedlock, she attempted to silence her baby's crying by covering his face over with a blanket. Unfortunately, this only caused him to become more distressed. Again she attempted to quieten the boys' screams and, in doing so, bashed his head against the side of the cot. Regrettably this action ended up killing the child and, ultimately, Elizabeth herself. During an investigation by Supernatural Investigations in 2009, one of the team members picked up on a woman crying in the corner of the basement cell. He questioned the story behind Elizabeth's demise, claiming that 'pieces didn't fit together'. He felt that it was a tragic accident and that Elizabeth should not have been executed.

Selina Wadge was a twenty-eight-year-old mother of two illegitimate sons. She was deeply impoverished and regularly had to rely on work from the Launceston Workhouse. Her two sons, Harry, aged two and John, aged six, were the apples of her eye and people from her home village later recalled that she would do anything for her children. Although Selina was single, she had met a man whom she was fond of in 1878. On 21 June 1878, Selina and her children hitched a ride with a farmer towards Launceston, apparently to meet her 'boyfriend'. The following afternoon she reached the workhouse with only one son, the oldest, John. When questioned by her sister, she claimed that her boyfriend had drowned Harry in a well at Altarnun on the previous evening. He then threatened to kill Selina and her eldest son, John. Harry's body was recovered from the well and after confessing to murdering Harry, Selina was remanded into custody. She claimed that her new boyfriend promised to marry her if she killed Harry. Unfortunately, regardless of her previous good character and her obvious love for her children, she was sentenced to death. Perhaps fortunate in some small way, she became the first person to be hanged using the 'Marwood method'. This meant that instead of being strangled to death she would be 'dropped' a measured distance so that her neck was broken. Her measured drop was calculated at 8 feet. This was also the first private execution away from public eyes – inside the wall of Bodmin Jail.

Selina's ghost has been seen wandering the prison reaching out to small children. Mark Rablin, the paranormal host at Bodmin, reports that children have been known to ask who the lady in the long dress crying is, and that pregnant women get very emotional on the third and fourth floor. Her ghost has also been witnessed as a full torso manifestation.

Supernatural Investigations have visited the jail twice since 2009. More recently, they were proud to attend a charity event hosted by Haunted Devon, where over £1,400 was raised. Perhaps the most intriguing part of the investigation for me was during a break between sessions in 2009. I decided that I would grab some long exposure shots of the Naval wing from inside. I retreated alone to the location, camera and tripod in hand, and set up inside the entrance. At 3 a.m. it was very dark and, being February, very cold. I lined up the shot, set the shutter to open for one minute and clicked away. During this period, I had time to be alone with my thoughts and my imagination. Being alone in the Naval wing is daunting to say the least; a chance to imagine shapes in dark corners and to misinterpret sounds as banshees wailing nearby. I glanced back at the camera and at that point I was struck on the head by a small pebble, which bounced off and rolled along the floor. Frozen to the spot for a second, I then looked up in an attempt to identify where the pebble had come from. It was at this point that I remembered that the roof of the Naval wing was missing and that a starry blue sky streaked above me. To the left and right were high walls and open cells surrounding me. With thirty seconds of exposure still to go, I began to feel a little anxious and was still puzzled as to where the stone had come from. My only assumption was that it was somehow projected from one of the cells three or four floors up. This thought only added to my fear as it was impossible for this to occur naturally. A deathly silence encompassed me as I waited for the final thirty seconds to finish and the picture to process.

Kev in the Naval wing with an unusual white streak of light to his left.

Bodmin Jail.

Supernatural Investigations and Haunted Devon pictured behind the last noose to be used at Bodmin Jail.

The noose and coffin, with the cross in the background.

Before I had chance to view the finished picture I clutched the tripod and camera and briskly left the area to re-join the rest of the team.

As paranormal investigators, we like to identify similarities in experiments over a period of time in a particular location. If we can record similar phenomena in one place on at least two separate occasions it then raises interesting questions as to the cause. It may not necessarily be paranormal in origin, but it does indicate there being something unusual. From here we can attempt to investigate the phenomena further and hopefully verify whether it is triggered by supernatural phenomena or by 'normal' environmental factors. One such event has occurred many times

at different intervals/days in the same location – the condemned man's cell. In 2009, Stuart Andrews and I were running a vigil in the mirrored cell when we began asking for a sign. Within minutes, our EMF (Electro-Magnetic Field) meter began spiking for a number of seconds before dropping out. It is worth bearing in mind that both Stuart and I had been alone in this room for at least ten minutes and during that time the EMF meter had been non-responsive. Each time Stuart asked a question, the EMF meter responded. In all other areas that evening the EMF did not behave in the same way.

In October 2011, Frances Roberts and I had the pleasure of holding a vigil in the same cell, again with an EMF meter.

An eerie figure in white can be seen here – is it a spirit or a living person captured on a slow shutter setting?

Lanhydrock House and gardens. (Photo courtesy of Simon Lewis, www.westcountryviews.co.uk)

During the thirty minutes we were in the cell the meter again responded to questions. In fact, later on that evening, Haunted Devon Training Manager Graham Chapman, Frances and I returned to the same cell with the EMF meter to attempt the same communication and, yet again, we were not disappointed. What caused it to spike remains unknown, but when we were silent, so was the meter. When we asked questions, the meter seemed to respond.

Bodmin Jail is an amazing location and is well worth a visit during daylight hours, or, if you dare, at night!

Lanhydrock House

Lanhydrock House is an exquisite Victorian mansion sitting in 890 acres of beautifully landscaped gardens near Bodmin. Parts of the house date back to the 1620s, when the estate was purchased by Sir Richard Robartes, a wealthy merchant. Following his death in 1624, the Robartes family continued to own the estate until it was passed over to the National Trust in 1953. In 1881, the house was damaged by fire, which destroyed the south wing of the property. Although no one was killed in the fire, Lady Robartes, who was rescued from the house, died a few days later in hospital, aged sixty-eight. Her husband died a year after losing his wife. It is believed that the spirit of Lady Robartes is often felt in 'Her Ladyship's Room'. Many visitors report the unmistakeable smell of cigar smoke in the Smoking Room, as though someone is actually smoking at that very moment.

Members of Supernatural Investigations had the pleasure of visiting Lanhydrock House in 2004. They ventured into the Smoking Room specifically to experience the phantom cigar smoke; although they stayed for quite some time they were not fortunate enough to smell the distinct aroma of tobacco. They did, however, notice that a curtain cord was swinging fairly violently on its own. The area was roped off behind a desk so the motion could not have been caused by the team, and the window was clasped shut. At one point the cord appeared to pick up pace before returning to a steady back and forth swinging motion.

The most well-known ghost at Lanhydrock House is that of the Grey Lady. She is a little old lady who has been seen walking between the Gallery and the Drawing Room. Visitors who have seen her explain that on first glance they think she is a real person, yet on approaching her she seems to disappear into thin air.

Maple Leaf Café

An inconsequential building located in Bodmin town centre became the location for one of the most frightening experiences in Michael Williams' forty years of paranormal investigating. In 2001, Michael and other members of the Ghost Club Society visited the former Maple Leaf Café on Honey Street in Bodmin, after a previous scouting assignment uncovered a sinister visitor at 4 p.m. most days. The spirit in question was often seen, but more regularly

heard climbing the staircase of the building. On the evening of the investigation, the Ghost Club's resident medium picked up on a soldier from the First World War, apparently returning to find his long-lost lover – his sister-in-law. The investigation took a turn when the medium's pendant, a tool used to communicate with the spirit world, swung violently in response to a question and the crystal broke free, striking Michael Williams, a senior Ghost Club Society member, in the face. It seemed the spirit did not favour the particular question and took offence. With a new pendant in use the same action occurred again, narrowly missing Michael's already wounded face.

The Green Frog Café, formerly the Maple Leaf Café on Honey Street, Bodmin.

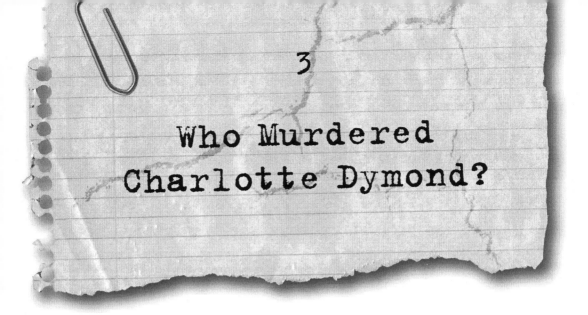

3

Who Murdered
Charlotte Dymond?

ON 23 April 1844, the body of a young woman was found face-upwards near a stream at the foot of Rough Tor. Her throat had been cut from ear to ear. Discovery of her body would spark a most intriguing and controversial investigation, and one that would see the largest gathering of people at a public hanging ever known. This is the tragic tale of Charlotte Dymond.

Knowledge of Charlotte's past is limited, with most details simply guess work. What we do know is that Charlotte was a vivacious eighteen-year-old maidservant working at Penhale Farm on Bodmin Moor. She was one of three live-in servants, along with John Stevens and Matthew Weekes, who all worked on the farm assisting the owner, Phillipa Peter and her son, John Peter. It is rumoured that Charlotte and Matthew were seeing each other and this relationship had been going on for eighteen months, before Charlotte worked at

the farm. Matthew himself had worked for Phillipa for over seven years and although he was a good farmhand, he had a physical disability that caused him to limp on his right leg. He was not blessed with good looks; with various top teeth missing, a thick brow and a pitted face, Matthew may well have wondered how he managed to secure the love of an attractive lass who was always smartly dressed. Charlotte herself was renowned for being a flirt and one such play for her affections was made by a twenty-six-year-old man called Thomas Prout. Thomas and Matthew knew each other well and were understandable enemies; they had worked together before and had not got along. Thomas was known to tease Matthew about Charlotte, saying that he would steal her away and that Matthew did not deserve her. He taunted Matthew. mentioning that he was going to move to Penhale Farm and that if this were

A wooded road near Rough Tor, possibly a familiar route that Charlotte would have taken back to Penhale Farm.

to happen, it would be inevitable that Charlotte and he would be together.

On Sunday, 14 April 1844, Thomas visited Charlotte at the farm and engaged her in conversation. The two were talking for a fair while before Thomas finally left. The conversation was witnessed by Matthew from a distance. Later that day, around 4 p.m., Charlotte and Matthew left the farm together wearing their Sunday best clothes. No one knew their destination; however, Charlotte mentioned that she would not be back in time to milk the cows that evening, but that Matthew would be. That fateful night, Charlotte did not return to the farm. The last confirmed sighting of Charlotte was later that evening by sixty-three-year-old farmer, Mr Isaac Cory. He had made his

way to Penhale Farm to see Phillipa, the owner, after attending the local church service at Davidstow. During the course of the evening he mentioned that he had seen both Charlotte and Matthew in the distance. He confirmed he knew it was Matthew due to his obvious limp and that Charlotte was wearing a green striped dress and red shawl; her outfit was corroborated by Phillipa. At this time nothing sinister was presumed and it was expected that Charlotte and Matthew would return later on that evening.

Matthew eventually returned alone, and, when questioned as to Charlotte's whereabouts, he answered that he did not know. At about 10.30 p.m. everyone except Phillipa went to bed. An hour later, after waiting up for Charlotte, she

Overcrowding would have been rife at Bodmin Jail, often leading to serious illness and death.

too bedded down for the night. Nine days later, Charlotte's body was found on the banks of the River Alan, near Rough Tor Ford. She was discovered by a party of twelve people, all local friends, neighbours and family who had stepped out purposely to look for Charlotte. They had followed footprints and marks in the mud, and had looked in locations where Charlotte and Matthew had last been seen together on that fateful Sunday night. Her body was eventually found about 12 inches from the water's edge; although dry, it was obvious that she had been in the water at some point, probably caused from the swell of the river. It is plausible that her body was washed downstream from what may have been the original murder scene. An unusual detail was the fact that various items she was wearing that Sunday evening were missing; items such as her shoes, her bonnet, handkerchief, bag, shawl and gloves. On examination, it was found that her neck wound was eight and a half inches in length and two and a half inches deep. It was suggested by the coroner that due to nick marks on her throat, the cut was not made in one long swoop, but that two clear cuts had been made.

Although Matthew was the prime suspect for the crime, he had left Penhale Farm three days before Charlotte's body was discovered. He had not told anyone of his destination and when a warrant was issued for his arrest, no one knew where Matthew was. The local constable traced Matthew's family and located his sister in Plymouth. Upon visiting her house, Matthew was found residing there and promptly arrested for the murder of Charlotte Dymond.

The trial began on 2 August 1844, at Bodmin Assize Court. Matthew entered a plea of 'Not Guilty' and the trial got under way. The trial lasted just twelve hours and, after thirty-five minutes of deliberation, the jury found Matthew Weekes 'Guilty' and he was sentenced to be hanged. On 12 August 1844, nearly four months to the day since the murder, Matthew was hanged in front of an unprecedented crowd of approximately 20,000 people before being laid to rest in the coal yard of Bodmin Jail.

The story itself has been researched, analysed and scrutinised many times over. The BBC even produced a dramatised documentary, which was screened on 1 January 1978. Although it would be fair to say that these events were not that rare at this time in England, it was uncommon to find such murderous acts in the rural communities enveloping Rough Tor and the neighbouring villages. The nature of the crime itself and the story of the love triangle between Charlotte, Matthew and Thomas only increased attention from media.

Pat Munn, local historian and author of *The Murder of Charlotte Dymond*, believes that there are a number of discrepancies with regard to the way the evidence was gathered, how it was collated, and the publicity of the trial itself. Certainly, Matthew was regarded as guilty long

Above *The grave at Davidstow Church, where Charlotte Dymond was buried.*

Left *The monument erected in memory of Charlotte Dymond, inscribed with the name of Matthew Weekes as 'Murderer'.*

before the trial began. This was demonstrated publicly with the placement of a monument to Charlotte at the site where her body was found. On it is inscribed:

This Monument erected by
Public Subscription in Memory of
Charlotte Dymond who was
Murdered by Matthew Weekes on
Sunday April 14th 1844.

The monument was erected a month before the murder trial even began, so Matthew was already deemed the murderer by the public and therefore any such trial would be erroneous. Pat mentions in her book that she thinks Matthew was innocent and that Charlotte had taken her own life based on the possibility that she was pregnant. Her book goes into some detail about the events leading up to the death and following the trial itself. There are a number of different arguments for and against Pat's conclusions, but what can be concluded is that such a trial would be executed very differently nowadays.

With the tragic nature of the crime, it is not hard to imagine that the event itself has been ingrained into the granite rocks and rugged landscape which surrounds the stream where Charlotte's body was found. It is known that the ghost of a woman has been seen on numerous occasions; a woman that appears one second and is gone the next. The following sightings are taken from Pat Munn's book, *The Murder of Charlotte Dymond*. The first is an account from a man staying at an old house called Tredethy in the early twentieth century. He claims that he was out walking by the River Alan, with the sun fairly low in the sky, and was following the stream in an attempt to avoid the marshland and make a safe return to his temporary abode. It was here, he claims, that he came across a young lady out alone, wearing 'a gown of different colours, a red cloth shawl and bonnet of silk'. It was as though she was 'looking for someone'. He was informed later that day that he had seen the ghost of Charlotte. It is reported that Cornwall Rifle Volunteers had camps near the base of Rough Tor at the end of the nineteenth century. 'Several of those who had been

posted alleged that they had seen the ghost of Charlotte crossing the moor'. To this day many fishermen returning from a day's fishing at the moorland streams claim to have seen a 'white figure' with her best clothes on.

It was a cold and miserable night in November 2011 when members of Supernatural Investigations attended the site of Charlotte's memorial. The area surrounding the memorial was boggy and the stream was flourishing with moorland springs. Although it had rained hard for hours before the investigation, we were given a respite from the elements for a short period of time. The wind was silent apart from the odd gust creaking through the nearby trees; however, it was enough to add a chill factor to an already icy evening. Looking up towards the stone formations at the top of Rough Tor, we questioned whether to climb the sodden grassland to the top, and, after a little deliberation, decided not to. We reported 'corner of the eye' phenomena as rock faces seem to come to life around us. Although we were alone, it felt as though we were at the centre of a group of people surrounding us – a rather eerie feeling to have late at night in the middle of the moor.

Once we had gathered our bearings I called out to Charlotte, asking her to communicate with us. Silence followed and we glanced at each other, wondering if any of us had heard anything. The electronic aids lay silent. I asked again for a sign and at that point the wind picked

As the sun sets over Rough Tor, the light turns the monument into a makeshift sundial.

up, rustling the trees and howling past the monument, before dying away to nothing. We stood silent for a few minutes before a loud hair-raising scream emanated in the distance. The hairs stood up on the back of my neck as one of the team members whispered, 'What the hell was that?' Again the scream ricocheted off the trees and through the air, this time much louder. 'What *is* that?' inquired another team member. I stated that it may be Charlotte in the grips of death, at which point the wind howled quite fiercely for a good five minutes.

Eventually the wind dropped and the clouds opened, emptying themselves of rain in one short burst. We gathered our electronic aids, now wet, and headed for the cars. Unfortunately, it continued to rain intensively for another hour and we decided it was no longer viable to continue the investigation. On reviewing the footage, I was able to capture the ear-splitting screams, which raised the hairs on my arms. Was it a recording of the murder of Charlotte Dymond? I would not like to speculate – it could very well have been a fox!

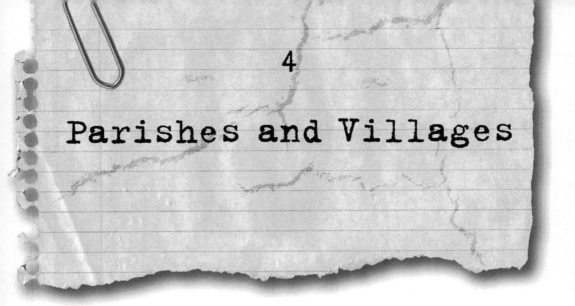

4

Parishes and Villages

BODMIN Moor is host to a number of parishes that stretch from south-east Cornwall all the way across to north Cornwall. Accessed from the south-east by the Draynes Valley, Bolventor sits on the border of the parishes of St Neot, Blisland and Alternun. Immediately to the north of Bolventor is the A30, one of only two main routes in and out of Cornwall. There are only a few buildings in this small settlement, one of which is the immortalised Jamaica Inn. I had the pleasure of driving through this hamlet following a paranormal investigation in North Devon in 2011. Apart from a few street and building lights, at 3.30 a.m. you are largely surrounded by a blanket of darkness. I stopped hesitantly to soak up the atmosphere and to take in the nexus of the settings and immediately I felt dread. It may have been the tiredness setting in after a long night's ghost hunting, but I felt an abrupt need to leave and drive home as fast as I could. Although

alone, I sensed I was being watched by a thousand eyes from the moor and that slowly they were making their way towards me. I quickly jumped back into my car and made my way home through the equally eerie Draynes Valley, constantly looking in my rear view mirror to make sure I was not being followed! Once through the valley and on to the St Cleer road, I released a sigh of relief and finally relaxed before reaching home and falling asleep safely in my bed. My summary, as a hardened ghost hunter, is that Bodmin Moor, in the dark, is not for the faint-hearted!

St Cleer

The first parish on the ghost tour of Bodmin Moor is St Cleer. Three miles north of my current hometown of Liskeard, St Cleer envelopes a major part of the moor between the A38 and the

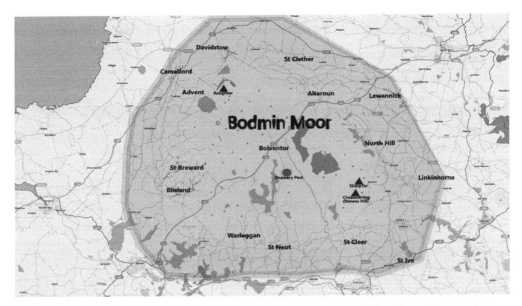

Map outlining the boundaries of Bodmin Moor and the parishes within. (Map © OpenStreetMap contributors, CC-BY-SA. www.openstreetmap.org)

A30, which are the two main routes in and out of Cornwall. The village of St Cleer sits at the base of the parish and was where I lived with my family until I was ten. It was also here that I experienced my first ghostly encounter, at just eight years of age. Ironically this experience did not happen in an old pub or near an ancient castle, but rather in my own home. At that time we lived at Valley View, just two doors down from one of only two pubs in St Cleer, the Stag Inn. My father used to frequent the Stag whilst I lay asleep in bed. On this particular occasion, I remember hearing my father coming home from a night of joviality and both my parents making their way to bed. I, too, eventually dropped off to sleep but later, during the night, I awoke parched for some

water. I called out to my mother, 'Mum! Mum!' and in an instant she arrived at my side. 'Please can I have some water?' I asked. I watched her as she turned on the landing light and descended the stairs to the kitchen. I lay waiting, dozing in and out of sleep. It appeared to take my mum a very long time to get a glass, fill it with water and return to my side and, at this point, I remember looking towards the end of my bed, where my bedroom window was. To my astonishment, I saw the figure of a woman looking out of my bedroom window, onto the street below. My curtains were drawn and the figure seemed to be standing in between the window and my bed, staring outwards. Assuming it was my mother, I called out and asked where my water was, to which there was no answer. I called again and asked the same question, and again to no avail. Upon questioning a third time I heard a noise from the staircase and watched in horror as my mum ascended the stairs with my glass of water. I gradually turned my head back towards the window, where, to my astonishment, the figure was gone. This memory stays clear in my mind to this day and it is one that will haunt me forever. But it was only the first in a number of unusual events I experienced in the five years that I lived in that house, but those stories are for another time!

The village itself is home to an ancient well, known as the 'Holy Well', which was built in the fifteenth century. It is a pleasant-looking granite well in lovely surroundings, but it has something of a lurid past. It is believed that this well was originally used as a bowsening pool, where the mad and insane were ducked in order to cure their 'illness'. The word 'bowsening', or 'bowse', is thought to come from the nautical term 'bouse', meaning to hoist or pull up with a tackle. These types of pools are apparently very rare; however, another bowsening pool exists on Bodmin Moor in the parish of Alternun. St Cleer's well is thought to be dedicated to St Clare, who was a twelfth-century disciple of St Francis. The well was knocked down during the Civil War and was not erected again until the nineteenth century, where it still stands proud and prominent in the village.

Around the corner from the well is the focal centre of the village – a thirteenth-century church and vicarage, which itself was the focus of an interesting story of

St Cleer Well, strangely resonant in time surrounded by modern-day buildings.

reincarnation that made the headlines in 1883. Reverend Hoskyns told the *Daily News*:

> A friend of mine, who is vicar of St Cleer, in east Cornwall, has told me that at least one housemaid of his — I think his servants in general — very anxiously avoided killing a spider, because Parson Jupp, my friend's predecessor (whom he succeeded in 1844), was, it was believed, somewhere in the vicarage in some spider — no one knew in which of the vicarage spiders.

On the outskirts of St Cleer, but still within the parish, are two ancient carved stones devoted to King Doniert. Although in ruin, it is thought that these stones were erected around the late ninth century and commemorated to Dumgarth, King of Dumnonia, who is thought to have drowned in a nearby lake. One of the stones is inscribed '*Doniert rogavit pro anima*', which is believed to translate as 'Doniert begs prayers for the sake of his soul'.

Further up the moor, near the small hamlet of Darite, lies an amazing rock formation called Trethevy Quoit, also known as King Arthur's Quoit — an impressive array of stones that form an enclosure thought to be a burial chamber. Standing at over 15 feet tall, it is thought this structure dates back to the Bronze Age and is known locally as 'the giant's house'.

A colleague of mine had seen a figure standing near Trethevy Quoit late one evening whilst parking his car near the entrance to the site. On leaving the vehicle, the figure had disappeared and, on investigation, was nowhere to be seen. The figure was described as dressed 'all in white' and seemed 'to glow' while standing by the stones. It was impossible for the figure to run away or hide in the short time it took my colleague to park the car, leaving him bemused as to what he had seen.

St Neot

Adjoining the parish of St Cleer is the village of St Neot. As you drive from St Cleer, passing King Donierts Stone, you will approach the Draynes Valley, a long stretch of single track country road that joins the south part of the moor to the A30, in the north. It is a daunting expanse of road to drive with many dips, troughs and blind corners, surrounded by woodland, stone walls, and not much else. It is not a place to end up alone at night, potentially miles from any human interaction, especially in the bleak, foggy winter months. Branching off this road is the infamous Golitha Falls, which we will touch upon later, however, the Draynes Valley has its own tale to tell. Two young men and two young women were travelling in one vehicle along the treacherous valley road one dark winter's night. They were heading towards the A30 at Bolventor and were travelling at some speed in an attempt to reach their

Part of the Draynes Valley that stretches from Redgate to Bolventor.

destination quickly. The night was clear and with little wind the journey was going smoothly until, quite suddenly, they turned a corner and were hit with a thick wall of fog. Slowing right down, they manoeuvred carefully ahead into the whiteness. Every so often the fog would lift and they had perfect visibility, but then were dropped into blindness once again. About half way through their journey, the driver swerved erratically and just missed leaving the road and ending up in a watery trough. After skidding to a halt, the car, having been filled with piercing screams, was stony silent. The occupants sat staring into the road, contemplating their near brush with death. The driver eventually broke the silence – 'Did you see that?' and was met with a

unanimously whispered, 'Yes'. The reason for the emergency manoeuvre was the appearance of a woman in white, wandering aimlessly along the desolate valley road. Although foggy, they had all seen the figure at the same time and she had appeared real enough to make the driver swerve to avoid hitting her. The same apparition has reportedly been seen on this road a number of times – it is thought that she is attempting to warn weary travellers of the dangers of this treacherous highway and to make them slow down.

A White Lady has purportedly been seen in the wondrous woodland of Golitha Falls. It is thought that because this area runs alongside the Draynes Valley that it is the same woman in white that haunts it. Golitha Falls is a woodland

Golitha Falls in the bleak mid-winter.

Golitha Falls further up river.

reserve that follows the River Fowey in its exciting white water descent through the valley gorge. It is a spectacular walk with a variety of colours, and creatures that support the surrounding environment. A popular area for dog walkers and a great place to cool off in the hot summer sun, thousands of visitors descend to Golitha Falls every year. As beautiful as it is during the day, at night it takes on a whole other persona. Night-time experiences include the sound of loud screams, heavy breathing, whispers when no one is there, and the sighting of a large black cat.

Probably the most impressive report of ghostly experiences from Golitha Falls is the sound of mining. Various people have described hearing metal tools bang against stone and a deep humming sound, so low in frequency it is almost difficult to hear but relays a definite feeling of unease. These reports have been noted at both night time and during the day. It is, therefore, not surprising to hear that Golitha was once used to mine copper and was aptly named Wheal Victoria Copper Mine. It is not clear whether anyone died during the mining years, but it is just possible that the mined granite may hold recordings of events since passed, which may be played to certain people as they venture through the rugged landscape.

Carnglaze Caverns sits on the main road from the A38 to the village of St Neot and is a man-made structure, formed as part of the slate quarry in the Loveny Valley. One of the three caverns is now used widely for concerts and by bands due to its exceptional acoustic atmosphere. Regardless of the temperature outside, the caverns maintain the same 10 degrees Celsius temperature all year around. Originally used in the Second World War by the Royal Navy to store large quantities of rum, it quite rightly earned the name 'The Rum Store'. When you wander deep into the caverns you gain a sense of respect for the miners that fought tirelessly to gouge the gaping holes in this amazing landscape of slate and, astonishingly, it seems there were no fatalities recorded at the caverns.

Many people who visit the caverns report the feeling of being watched from the far corners, as well as hearing the sound of slate being chipped away using a metal tool. Although paranormal reports are at a minimum, some people who experience the ambience and serenity of the caverns also report having an enlightened supernatural experience from within, an unearthly reflection of their soul. The caverns are indeed surrounded by magical tales of Faeries and King Arthur, and this helps the fantasy world that the caverns offer deep within.

Near Coliford lake, near the top of the parish of St Neot, is Dozmary Pool. A picturesque expanse of water, it is also the focus for two separate mystical tales of old. It was here that Sir Bedivere followed King Arthur's request and threw Excalibur into the lake while the king lay dying at the shore. The Lady of the Lake is believed to haunt the rustic moorland pool.

The London Inn and church at St Neot.

lake was infinitely deep; however, such ideas were dismissed after the pool dried up in the late nineteenth century. The pool still exists but is now much smaller than it once was.

St Neot is a little hamlet sheltered from the rough moorland winds by hills on three sides. As well as being home to the popular London Inn, it is host to a fifteenth-century church and a holy well. Legend has it that St Neot himself was praying by the well when an angel came to him and showed him three fishes in the well. He was told never to take more than one fish and he obeyed for some time. Unfortunately, on one occasion he fell ill and Barius, his servant, was entrusted to retrieve the fish from the well. Unbeknownst to St Neot, Barius had plucked two fish and had promptly cooked them. On bringing them to St Neot, he was ordered to immediately return the two fish to the well. Upon returning them to the waters of the well, the fish miraculously came to life and continued swimming.

As well as the legend of King Arthur, the ghost of Jan Tregeagle has been seen sitting beside the lake screeching like a wraith. The wind is said to carry his screams across the pool and far beyond to warn others of his atrocities. Banished to the lake for eternity, he was tasked to empty the lake with only a limpet shell. To make sure he kept busy and didn't wane in his duty, a pack of headless hounds chase him around the pool, snapping at his heels. It was thought that the

Altarnun

The village of Altarnun is cut in half by the A30 but features prominent moorland on either side. Altarnun sits close to Five Lanes and both contain historic inns – the King's Head and the Rising Sun. Altarnun itself is a mysterious place and seems to offer unusual activity in the area surrounding the church. The church itself was host to a deacon called Peter, who was reported to have been a hideous man in character. He was always out for his own ends and treated the sacred sanctity of the church as a playground for his antics. His foul behaviour was highlighted by his act of digging up the dead, so that he could steal from the recently departed. Some thought his actions to be of a more 'satanic' nature, so that he could bring about 'everlasting life' for himself. Over time he earned the nickname Peter Jowle (Joule) or 'Peter the Devil', however, at the age of 100, he was a frail, grey-headed, toothless man. Although this seemed to ridicule opinions of his devilish nature for everlasting life, it was recounted that at this time people noticed new black hairs growing on his scalp and teeth emerging in his mouth. He apparently lived to be 150 years old.

Next to the church is Penhallow Manor, an old rectory which was built in 1842 by Reverend Tripp. Penhallow Manor is not the original house on the site. It is thought that an original structure built in the sixteenth century initially took place where the new manor is but was burnt to the ground in unknown circumstances. The word Penhallow is thought to mean 'on the edge of the moor' and Altarnun is certainly that. The manor itself has links to the infamous Jamaica Inn at Bolventor. Although legend has it that Daphne du Maurier stayed at Penhallow Manor, perhaps to gain inspiration for her novel, *Jamaica Inn*, I have it on good authority that this was not the case. The old rectory, however, does feature in the book, playing the role of the home for the notorious Francis Davey, the vicar of Altarnun. As a rectory it homed many a vicar before

Dozmary Pool looks like the water has risen considerably in recent months.

Penhallow Manor, with the church steeple visible in the background.

being transformed into a hotel in the mid-twentieth century. After he died, Reverend Tripp was buried in the nearby church graveyard, yet poignantly, he was not buried alongside his wife but next to another woman called Mary Hurley, who is believed to have been his housekeeper. Reports of a ghostly woman wandering the corridors and land around Penhallow are believed to be that of Mary herself. Possibly the same woman has been seen on many occasions standing at the back door of the house by different people, yet when they look again, she is gone. It is thought that Mary may have been more than just a housekeeper to the Reverend and that is why they are buried together.

Marie, a previous owner of the hotel, has seen the spectre of a woman on the stairs and heard strange noises and footsteps when nobody has been on the premises except herself. A guest at the manor reported seeing a woman standing at the end of her bed wearing a Quaker's outfit. This spirit manifested itself for several minutes before disappearing into thin air. Harry Cleverley, a local psychic, was called in to investigate the manor after reports of disembodied footsteps were heard above the lounge area of the house. He recounted seeing a man in a Reverend's cloth walking back and forth between rooms 3 and 4, with his arms behind his back. It is understood that originally these rooms would have been a single room, making an office or bedroom. Harry mentions that it seemed as though the figure was pondering upon a sermon for the coming Sunday service at the local church. Mr Cleverley has also described an encounter he had outside the manor whilst walking his dog one evening. In the documentary *Ghosthunters – Spirits of Bodmin Moor*, Harry describes a close encounter with a floating entity. Both he and his dog were frozen to the spot as the spirit moved through the Penhallow gates, passed him, over the bridge and up the road before disappearing. His story was later confirmed by someone else who had seen the same thing on a different night. Research has shown that there was swampland originally behind the post office and that a woman had drowned there. It is thought that the ghostly midnight figure is the spirit of the poor lass that succumbed in the marsh.

The same figure was witnessed years later by Phil Bate and Antonio Rossi. One evening, after leaving the Rising Sun pub down the road from Altarnun village, the two men jumped into their car to drive the long journey home. They were chatting away happily when they approached the village and the old rectory. At this point they overtook what appeared to be a woman 'floating' down the road and over the old bridge at Altarnun. They both turned around to take a second look, but the figure was gone – she had simply vanished into thin air.

The hotel was owned recently by Mr and Mrs Nash, who, although never experiencing any spooky events themselves, were aware of some unusual things occurring in the manor. Mr Nashs's dog

Approaching the village of Altarnun from the A30 at Five Lanes.

would never enter the property – only ever advancing as far as the door and looking in, before moving away with his tail between his legs. On many occasions they attempted to coax him in with food and treats but he would not budge across the threshold. Staff members would not feel comfortable in the back area when dressing down the room and making the beds, often feeling as though they are being watched. Several times after the beds were made, on inspection, the covers had become ruffled and the pillows indented, indicating that someone had been present in the room. This didn't happen in all the quarters but was a regular occurrence in the back room. On one occasion, a group of women on a hen do came down from London to reside at the hotel. After being given their keys, one particular lady re-entered reception and requested another room. On questioning, she simply answered that she felt uncomfortable in that room; that she didn't feel as if she was alone in it. This was the same room that has caused problems for staff previously.

As with St Cleer, Altarnun has its own 'Bowsening pool'. The well is dedicated to St Nonna (Nona), who is thought to have been the Earl of Cornwall's daughter. According to Carew and Borlase in *The Legendary Lore of the Holy Wells of England* by Robert Charles Hope (1893), the process for curing insanity was as follows:

The water running from this sacred well was conducted to a small square enclosure closely walled in on every side, and might be filled at any depth, as the case required. The frantic person was placed on the wall, with his back to the water; without being permitted to know what was going to be done, he was knocked backwards into the water, by a violent blow on the chest, when he was tumbled about in a most unmerciful manner, until fatigue had subdued the rage which unmerited violence had occasioned. Reduced by ill-usage to a degree of weakness which ignorance mistook for returning sanity, the patient was conveyed to church with much solemnity, where certain Masses were said for him. If after this treatment he recovered, St Nun had all the praise; but in case he remained the same, the experiment was repeated so often as any hope of life or recovery was left. The mystic properties of this well have been transferred by the vulgar to the Pixies, whose goodwill is obtained by an offering of a pin.

Warleggan

Carved between Cardinham and St Neot is the parish of Warleggan. A mostly barren landscape with little human inhabitation, it was once thought to be the most remote area in Cornwall. The village itself consists of just a handful of houses, a church and a chapel. Twinned with C.S. Lewis' fictional Narnia, Warleggan certainly has the feeling of stepping into another world. The local church is where our story begins. Since the fourteenth century, St Bartholomew's Church has been plagued with stories of ghosts and witchcraft. In 1334, Ralph de Tremur, son of the second Rector of St Bartholomew's, left the village denouncing the idiosyncrasies of faith and religion before returning to the village and promptly burning down the rectory. He was thought to have been a practising witch and was brought before the Bishop in Exeter, who berated him with the following phrase:

> O detestable tongue, more poisonous than that of a mad dog which ought to be cut out by the surgeons of the Church and Crown and be chopped up and thrown to the pigs.

Perhaps the most famous character in the story of St Bartholomew's is Reverend F.W. Densham, rector of Warleggan from 1931 until his death in 1953, aged eighty-three. An interesting character, his vision of how a rectory should look startled a number of parishioners. Laura Farnworth puts forth the scene in *The Story of Reverence Densham*:

> Within the old rectory big red crosses are painted upon most of the upstairs doors. Upon each cross is written, in capital letters, a Biblical name, such as Pizgah, Emmaus and Cyprus. Bolts are fixed on the outside of the doors while some of the windows bear as many as five catches.

St Bartholomew's and possibly the Revd Densham from 1953. (Gift of the Estate of Carl Mydans, 2005)

> The crosses and their names are cracked and darkened, but vivid still; and the rows of catches are there also. Densham, himself, created the strange scene.

Due to the Reverend's eccentric actions, he lost his parishioners and ended up preaching to cardboard cut-outs – propped up in the pews – for over twenty years. Such actions made Densham a very lonely man and although he tried to make amends by building a children's playground and decorating his three spare rooms for visitors, no one ever used either. Some blame his odd behaviour on his close relationship with Ghandi in the 1920s, who was a major influence in his life. Whilst working in India on one of the tea plantations, he was open to various teachings from Ghandi himself and it is thought that this was the reason that he became a vegetarian.

Once news got out about this unconventional character, Densham became an international celebrity overnight. Reporters from all over the world flocked to the little village of Warleggan to get a glimpse of this strange man and his cardboard congregation.

Densham's ghost has been seen on many occasion drifting along the path to the vicarage and it is also believed that he haunts the rectory, which has now been converted into modern flats. On one occasion two people had their photograph taken outside the rectory and, when the picture was developed, there was a third person in the background. Even though it was determined that there was no other person around at the time, a man is clearly seen looking at the camera.

In 1999, Michelle Haines recounted her experience:

> On four occasions this year I've been aware of a dark presence, nothing menacing despite the darkness, and twice it has stroked my arm. Not in a threatening or sexual way. It was rather reassuring and I am certain it was the spirit of Mr Densham. I was also aware of his presence when I was picking apples in the grounds. He seems drawn to me.

Linkinhorne

To the north-east of St Cleer is the parish of Linkinhorne. While Linkinhorne itself does not seem to boast many stories of spectres, the village of Minions does. As well as finding one of the highest pubs in Cornwall, The Cheesewring Hotel, you will also find one of the main sighting areas for UFO's and stories of the infamous Beast of Bodmin Moor. Minions is also home to mystical stone arrangements such as the Hurlers and the Cheesewring itself. The Cheesewring is believed to be a geological formation of rocks weathered over time into an outcrop of granite slabs. Its name derived from a press-like device that was once used to make cheese. As with many strange formations on the moor, legend has a fabulous story for the creation of the Cheesewring. A long, long time ago, before Christianity donned the isle of Britain, giants lived unchallenged on the moor. They were reliant on the local people to bring them provisions, like slaves upon request. Before long, the saints descended on Cornwall and began claiming wells and naming them 'holy'. The giants felt this was an act of war and named Uther, one of the giants, as their leader. He was tasked to rid the saints from the land and protect the locals from their 'idiotic' beliefs. St Tue, an old and frail man, overhead this judgement and decided to challenge Uther to a test of strength in a rock-throwing contest. Uther was the champion giant at this game and thought this contest was a sure thing in favour of the giants. He laid down the gauntlet, and rules were that the losers would leave the land never to return. St Tue agreed and the competition began. Each contestant was required to gather twelve round, flattish stones to be flung. Uther went first, throwing a small-ish rock onto Stowes Hill, where it lay perfectly. St Tue, a lot smaller and weaker, prayed to God to give him strength and to help him in his mission. With this belief he lifted a fairly heavy rock with ease and flung the stone onto the surface of the first. It balanced perfectly and the saints cheered with delight. The competition continued until, at twelve stones apiece, Uther threw his thirteenth stone. As it struck the top of the formation of stones it rolled off the top and down the hill. It was now up to St Tue to finish the competition and claim overall victory – if he could just place the thirteenth stone perfectly on top. Again he prayed to the heavens and with that an angel appeared before him. The angel took the rock from his hands and placed it on top of the pile of stones, giving triumph to the saints. From there on Uther vowed to denounce his evil ways and the saints continued to live on and around Bodmin Moor.

The Hurlers hold an equally interesting story in folklore. Some people believe they were erected by druids; however, the locals have a far more interesting story for their presence. Deep in the vaults of time the various parishes enjoyed playing hurling on Craddock Moor against each other. Hurling was a popular pastime played in Cornwall and is likened to a primitive form of

The Hurlers at Minions.

rugby, with a small silver ball. The locals enjoyed playing this sport so much they played it as often as they could, including on the Sabbath. The locals of St Cleer began to annoy the saint himself when, come the Sabbath, his church was empty. Whilst sitting and looking at his vacant pews he could hear the distant cheers and chants of his flock playing the game on the moor. One day this angered him so much that he approached his parishioners during the game and forbade them from playing the game on a Sunday again. For a while it seemed to work and his worshippers returned to Sunday service, but the good fortune for St Cleer did not last. When once again his church was empty he took his staff and walked up to the moor. Full of rage he offered his flock a final ultimatum – to return to his church, or else! Some of the flock obeyed and returned while others, defiant, stayed. He raised his staff and told them that if they loved the game so much then they would stay on the moor forever, before lowering his staff hard on the ground. To the horror of the spectators, all the hurlers were turned to stone. To this day the weathered granite still stands tall on Craddock Moor.

Minions is also home to Daniel Gumb's Cave. He was an eighteenth-century stone-cutter and amateur mathematician. Originally, his home was further over to the base of Stowes Hill but this was moved to make way for the quarry that now exists. It was carefully dismantled and moved but no longer represents the sizeable property it once was. Cleverly, Daniel managed to create a home from the large granite slabs and tunnelled below to make three sizeable rooms. The roof slab alone measured 30 feet by 10 feet and was the main canopy against the blistering moorland weather. Daniel married at least three times and here managed to raise nine children. You may think that, between his long hours as a stone-cutter and helping to raise all his children, he would not have time for anything else; however, Daniel was a keen mathematician and had managed to teach himself fairly complex mathematics. It is said that he used to watch the stars at night, which helped him with his calculus. The carving of Euclid's Theorem is clearly seen etched on the roof of his cave: a stone near the entrance to the cave bears the carved inscription 'D GUMB 1735'. It is understood that this represents the date of his third marriage. Amazingly, despite the harsh moorland living, Daniel lived to the ripe age of seventy.

St Breward

Deep in the heart of Bodmin Moor lays St Breward. A small community, it has its fair share of interesting tales. St Breward is home to the Old Inn, an appealing pub and restaurant located next to the highest church in Cornwall, standing at about 700 feet above sea level. The Old Inn also claims to be the highest inn in Cornwall and is over 200 years old.

Hurlers in the foreground with Stowes Hill and the Cheesewring in the background.

Marriage memorial stone outside Daniel Gumb's Cave.

King Arthur's Hall near St Breward. (Photo courtesy of Simon Lewis © www.westcountryviews.co.uk)

Legend has it that, with an offering of pins, the water in St Breward's Well can cure sore eyes. The holy well is hidden away from the main part of the village and, sadly, I was unable to find it on my visit. I certainly would have sore eyes if I had kept looking for the mysterious structure.

In the centre of the village is a community hall, where the ghost of a little girl has been seen on occasion. She is a playful little lass who likes to get involved with the local playgroup. It is understood that when they attempt to count the number of children in the group, each

time they add up, it becomes a different figure. They believe that the young ghost pretends to be part of the group and causes the miscalculation.

The legend of King Arthur strateches far and wide across Cornwall and St Breward has its connections to the infamous King as well. Slightly north of Leaze Farm, near the De Lank River, is a megalithic structure known as King Arthur's Hall. These are fifty-six granite stones arranged in a rectangular format around a marshland area which regularly fills with water. It is thought that at one stage there were over

140 of these stones, all standing no more than 2 meters high. Reason for this structure is unknown, but it is thought that it dates back prior to 1584, when it was first documented. Unfortunately, due to cattle, the site has become greatly damaged.

On a more supernatural note, I was informed of a particular private house in the village which was said to have a poltergeist-type resident. A number of years ago a family were forced from their home because of strange goings-on inside. Door knobs would rattle on their own, light bulbs would blow up and ornaments and other household items would be flung across the room. Over time this became too much for the family and they called in some Christians to pray over the house. The outcome of this action is unknown, but since that period the residents have moved out and the house is believed to have become occupied again.

5

The Secrets of Davidstow Airfield and War Museum

IGH up on Bodmin Moor in the parish of Davidstow is a large flat area of moorland that spreads out for miles. In the distance you can see the peaks of Rough Tor and the treeline that encompasses Davidstow woods, behind which lies Crowdy Reservoir, a large expanse of open water. The main road that joins the A30 to the A39, towards Camelford, is long and straight and offers magnificent views. There are times you almost feel like you are floating over the road as opposed to driving along it; a very surreal experience. What significantly enhances this landscape are the abandoned buildings that are dotted around the barren moor; old units from the days of war supporting the airfield that hides in plain sight around you. It is not until you see an aerial photograph that you come to appreciate the strange shapes that make up the airfield itself.

It is clear to see the various take-off and landing segments, but what makes it peculiar are the numerous circular stalks that lead off from the main concrete segments. Like a 1970s fractal diagram, they branch out poignantly like stems on a plant. Nowadays the airfield is but a shadow of its former self, mainly used for light aircraft and enthusiastic teenagers hijacking their parents' cars for a brief experience at driving in a fairly safe environment. I say fairly safe as I was once one of those teenagers. At just fourteen years of age, my father allowed me to take control of his car on the now-derelict ground that used to make up the main runway. A brave man, he sat helplessly as a passenger as I attempted to learn the concept of driving. Things went well until we noticed in the distance a light aircraft heading our way, coming in to land. Panicking, we quickly switched seats and drove off at speed, away from the incoming plane.

At fourteen I was unaware of the history of this amazing location and

Photo taken from the top of Rough Tor, overlooking Bodmin Moor and nearby Davidstow.

certainly did not realise it was haunted. In November 2011, Supernatural Investigations were treated to an all-night investigation here. We were warmly welcomed by the resident paranormal group, Soul Searchers, who took us on a tour and showed us the hotspots. Soul Searchers have been actively investigating both this airfield and the Cornwall at War Museum since 2009. They have captured various anomalous phenomena on digital recording devices – from freaky photos to strange voices, and we had high hopes that we could do the same.

The airfield officially opened on 1 October 1942, and served as a fully operational RAF station until it was closed in December 1945. Its primary function was to act as 'Coastal Command' to the Royal Navy and to protect convoys from the German U–Boat force, also known as the Wolfpacks. Another function was to protect allied shipping from aerial threats posed by the Luftwaffe. Three runways were built, each at least 1,400 yards long, with one runway measuring 2,000 yards. Over 300 officers served at this station, employing several types of aircraft during the three years that the airfield was open, including the Lockheed Hudson, an American–built bomber and coastal reconnaissance aircraft used in 1943 and 1944; the Bristol Beaufighter, a British long–range heavy fighter; the Supermarine Walrus; Vickers Warwick and Vickers Wellington, another British long–range medium bomber, and, finally, the Hawker Henly, a two–seater target tug based on the Hawker Hurricane.

Unfortunately, Davidstow airfield witnessed a number of disasters in the three years it was operational. It is reported that approximately forty aircraft crash–landed at the airfield after

The Soul Searchers team and Kayleigh sit patiently in the Officers' Mess.

being out on a mission. Many were in trouble following action and could not land safely, while others overshot the runway, probably due to technical issues, and it is reported that over 100 aircrew personnel lost their lives whilst protecting us from the German enemy.

On the evening of 9 December 2011, my colleague, Kayleigh Williams, and myself were fortunate to be invited along to investigate the Cornwall at War Museum with the host group, Soul Searchers, led by paranormal investigator, Bev. The night was cold but that did not stop me from wearing shorts. The sky was clear, crisp and bright, with a full moon illuminating the sky; that was until we arrived at the location. In the space of ten minutes the wind gathered pace, clouds

rolled in and torrential rain poured down. Within another ten minutes the clouds were gone, the wind was still and the sky was once again bright and clear, which is how it stayed for the rest of the night. We were met by Bev and taken to the tea and snack cabin, where we were showered with hot drinks and a selection of chocolates, biscuits and sandwiches; an excellent start to the evening, I thought. Bev soon revealed each location to us within the museum itself, gently caressing our minds with facts about what has been known to occur here, and we were excited about the evening ahead.

We started off the evening in the Officers' Mess: Bev and her team and Kayleigh and I sat around a table after setting up all the equipment. A small filter of natural light entered the room, allowing low visibility. Ironically, even though there were around ten people in the room, we all had the feeling that we were surrounded. We also sensed movement in the corners, yet each time I moved towards an area where we thought the renowned 'shadow man' was, he appeared to move to a different corner. It was as if I was chasing him around the room. On a number of occasions certain team members felt as though someone had rushed past them, in and out of the room. Bev told us that a gentleman officer has been seen in this room and that he is keen on the ladies. On the night, he appeared to take a shining to our new budding investigator, Kayleigh. On various occasions she was touched or could feel warm breath on her neck when no one was close. On Bev's request, I set up a camera in the hall, next to some artefacts and mannequins behind a glass shield. Bev had told me that this area was prone to activity and that sometimes artefacts are found in different places from where they were left. On viewing the footage on the digital camcorder, I was disappointed to see that nothing had moved; however, I was immediately intrigued to hear what sounded like a man groaning. The sound was very unusual in that it seemed to move past the camera from left to right, although nothing appeared visually in the footage. What made this more interesting was that whatever had made the sound would have been moving along the corridor towards the Officers' Mess. At this

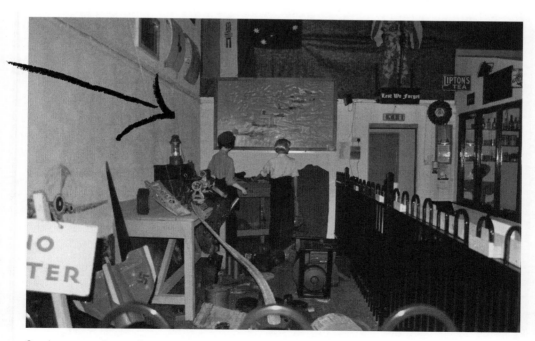

Spooky mannequins watch on as we prepare to encounter the unknown.

time all of Bev's team, Kayleigh and I were *in* the Officers' Mess. At the end of the footage we can be heard quite clearly walking towards and past the camera. The groaning sound was not accompanied by the sounds of footsteps or physical movement – it was as though the groan was floating through the air and not 'walking' past the camera.

Our next stop was in the ballroom area of the museum, an old hangar-shaped building with more artefacts and more eerie mannequins. The room we started in was adjacent to the ballroom itself and seemed a lot cooler to start with. Although we were investigating in December, I was surprised to notice how much colder this area was compared to the Officers' Mess. The smell of burning flesh has been noted in this location on more than one occasion. Unfortunately, at this time we were not privy to such a smell, however, we did hear some unusual sounds emanating from the back of the room itself. On inspection, I could not find any visitors or rodents that may have snuck in under the light of the moon. This area also played havoc with my equipment and I was forced to replace batteries in my voice recorder three times during the one-hour session. I had charged and checked all batteries before the investigation, as any hardened technological ghost-hunter would do. Ironically, in all other areas, this did not seem to be a problem. Kayleigh reported feeling uncomfortable in this room, as though she were being watched.

Further into the vigil, Mark Rablin, resident medium at Bodmin Jail and also a member of the Soul Searchers group, said that he could smell woodbine cigarettes. When I moved into that area, there was definitely a strong smell of smoke, yet no one was smoking. Within a few minutes the smell was gone and we were left baffled as to what had caused it.

We then entered the ballroom itself and were met with a very creepy scene. The room was laid out with tables and chairs strewn down the centre of the room, with five or six male mannequins dotted around the hall dressed in bow ties and jackets. On a dark, cold, winter's night in a haunted location, this set up is quite unnerving. At first the room felt calm and comfortable, however, the atmosphere soon turned frosty and unwelcoming. We kept seeing shadow play in one of the corners, as though a tall, dark man was staring out at us. I moved towards the offending area and was surprised to find the temperature a lot cooler when I got there; it was as though I had walked straight into a cold spot. I felt a little uneasy and could feel what seemed to be someone or something touching my head – causing me to immediately move away from this location. I decided to walk up and down the room on the far side of the tables to see if I could sense anything unusual. At one point, a member of the team shouted out that they could see a dark shadow following me. I reached the end of the room, turned around and walked back

Outside the ballroom, where the distinct smell of woodbine has been detected.

and, all of a sudden, was pushed into the tables and chairs. I stood up but no one was there! I cannot explain it but I was definitely pushed over. This was a very discomforting experience but it captured my full interest and I was intrigued to see what else this 'shadow man' could do. It soon became evident that this was probably the same man seen in the Officers' Mess, and the two rooms are connected. We sat quietly for a bit and called out but we did not get a response. Our time was up and the team decided it was time for tea and biscuits back at the base room, but I was still shaken by my experience and wanted to do another ten minutes or so in this area. Kayleigh, although on her first investigation, agreed to stay with me. We continued to attempt to make

contact with any spirits in the location, but again we were disappointed with the results. Just before we decided to join the others back at base room, both Kayleigh and I heard a loud bang in the next room. It sounded like a door slamming shut and within seconds I was on my feet with a torch in hand; off to find what I thought would be another team member returning for something they had forgotten. I left the ballroom and moved towards where I thought the sound had come from, but no one was there. I tried opening and closing the doors but they did not match the sound that we had heard. It was at this point that I realised that I had left Kayleigh alone in the ballroom. I soon returned and she was fine, although a little scared.

The ballroom, with more mannequins to help make the atmosphere more unnerving.

While we were in the ballroom area we tried some ovilus work to attempt communication with any spirits that may have wished to speak out. An ovilus is a device that uses multiple sensors to detect variations in EMF waves in the air. It contains a database of over 10,000 words and the theory is that a spirit can manipulate the waves and therefore affect speech by choosing a certain word from the device catalogue. Unfortunately, we only had the smart phone application version of the ovilus and, as such, any results should be taken with a pinch of salt. Needless to say, I have been on investigations where the word selection was uncannily accurate to the scenario and theme of questions we were asking. That night at the Cornwall at War Museum was to be one of the most accurate ovilus experiences I have ever had. One of Bev's team members also had the same phone application on her device and we decided to run them together to see what correlation we could make. We left them running and began questioning by calling out, and it was not long before we got some responses. It appeared as though there was more than one spirit in our location and they were keen to talk to us. Both devices began churning out words frequently and most, if not all, the words were connected to our location and in relation to the military. The word 'state' was followed closely by 'subversion'. 'Coast' trailed shortly after, which was ironic, as Davidstow was used primarily as coastal support. 'June' was a response to a question about an important date in time; we feel this was related to the D-Day landings on 6 June 1944. 'Military', 'Escape', 'Spain', 'Europe', 'Community' and 'Officer' were other words that were linked, maybe loosely, but significantly to Davidstow RAF base. People often question whether there is any validity in the responses that the ovilus gives out and I am the first person to question such responses, however, I test the replies by considering whether the same words would be applicable to another location, for instance a pub. In this case I think it would be hard to relate the words we received to another location. Perhaps the most intriguing part of the evening was when my ovilus device said in quick succession 'purple' then 'flower'. At the same time the other ovilus device said 'blue' then 'flower'. We sat confused for a while before we realised that it may be associated with squadron colours. We immediately made our way to the corridor by the Officers' Mess, where all the squadron colours could be found on the walls. We desperately looked for a blue/purple flower and what we found was truly amazing. On the wall was a picture of a blue/purple thistle which belonged to 236 Squadron. We then asked the ovilus where information on this squadron could be found, to which the ovilus replied 'west'. We worked out which way was west and headed in that direction – on the wall

at the end of the corridor hung all the information about that particular squadron. Finally, the ovilus made one more startling announcement; it mentioned the word 'drown' and, upon reading through the squadron information, we discovered that two members had drowned when their plane had gone down in the sea. The frequency and timing of the words were amazingly accurate considering it is simply a database of 10,000 unique words that may be picked at random. If this is the case and there is absolutely no connection between spirit manipulation and the device, then this was the most precise case of coincidence I have ever witnessed. I was certainly taken aback by this incredible period of activity.

I was keen to ask Bev about her many experiences at Davidstow and whether she was successful in capturing any evidence worthy of analysis. She pointed me in the direction of the Soul Searchers website (www.soulsearcherskernow.com) and asked me to listen to their EVPs (Electronic Voice Phenomena) section. On returning home, this was the first thing I did and I was amazed to hear some of the voices they managed to capture on a device called 'Frank's Box'. Basically, this is an untuned radio that skips through all the various radio stations at speed on a particular frequency, such as FM or AM. This happens over and over and it this thought that communication could be initiated with the spirit world by utilising the white noise and short bursts of tuned stations as they pass through.

Again, it could be argued that this device gushes out random phrases or parts of words that are purely coincidental responses to questions posed, however, I was surprised at some of the responses that the Frank's Box gave to certain questions posed by the Soul Searchers team. There are currently nineteen different EVPs to listen to on the website and it will be for you to make your own mind up whether you believe the phenomena to be purely coincidental or really the voices of the deceased reacting to questions from the living.

Davidstow airfield is certainly an amazing location and is probably one of the moor's best kept paranormal secrets, with only a handful of groups honoured enough to have experienced an all-night investigation here. Although my team, Supernatural Investigations, were unable to join me that evening, I know that they are certainly interested in booking a future investigation at the airfield. I will be delighted to be offered the opportunity to explore the barren outbuildings and museum area of Davidstow. Perhaps the fog-ridden landscape where the airfield lies is the perfect scene for the spirits that roam the moor, or could it be that with such a suggestible backdrop it is inevitable that paranormal experiences will be reported? Either way, Davidstow is an astounding place to visit.

Many thanks to Bev and her team at Soul Searchers for their hospitality and leadership on the evening.

6

Jamaica Inn

LOCATED in the small hamlet of Bolventor, Jamaica Inn is a solitary public house and hotel very close to the A30. Built in the 1750s, it was a coaching house on the main route from London to Cornwall. Before Bodmin became the location of an assize court, the main route was regularly used by Justices of the Peace on their way to Launceston, and the inn became an attraction on route. The inn was also a regular stop for mail coaches, which often used the coaching route to ship mail up and down the country. However, Jamaica Inn has a more notorious history as a haunt for smugglers.

The inn became a popular place for storing stolen contraband, mainly due to its solitary location – being surrounded entirely by moorland. The name 'Jamaica Inn' was thought to have been used because of the smugglers bringing in vast quantities of 'Jamaican Rum' and storing it at the inn. It is actually known, however, that the name originates from the Trelawney family, landowners who had two family members who served as Governors of Jamaica in the eighteenth century.

Daphne du Maurier as she would have looked when writing her bestselling novel, Jamaica Inn. (© The Chichester Partnership)

Front of the popular smuggler's haunt, Jamaica Inn.

The inn was immortalised by the late Daphne du Maurier in 1936. Born in London in 1907, she was the middle daughter of prominent actor-manager, Sir Gerald du Maurier. With her grandfather, who was also an author, it was no surprise that Daphne followed in the family footsteps. In 1931, she published her first novel, *The Loving Spirit*. After staying at the inn three years earlier, Daphne penned one of her greatest novels of all time, *Jamaica Inn*. It was a fictional piece of work about a twenty-three-year-old woman named Mary Yellan. Mary moves to the inn to live with her aunt and uncle after her mother dies and, upon arrival, soon realises that her 7-foot tall uncle is a tyrant and a bully. The uncle, who is also the innkeeper, turns out to

be the leader of a band of wreckers and as events unfold Mary becomes wise to some awful acts performed by her uncle. This book was later produced as a film by director Alfred Hitchcock, yet this differed from the book in many respects and it was reported that Daphne du Maurier was not pleased with the end production.

Although Jamaica Inn is renowned for its part in Daphne du Maurier's book, it is no surprise that it has a reputation of its own that has attracted media attention from all over the world. With most inns that are a few hundred years old, it is understandable that stories of unusual happenings should be reported, with myths and legends that get twisted and changed through the ages. Jamaica Inn has its fair share of ghost stories and paranormal activity that has assumed it the title of one of the most haunted inns in Britain – so much so that television-based paranormal productions have flocked to the inn to perform their own investigations. On 6 April 2004, Living TV's *Most Haunted* aired an episode of their investigation at Jamaica Inn. The team described the location as one of the spookiest places they have ever visited. One of the scenes shows the team scaring themselves and running out of the generator room screaming. The generator room is now the new reception at the inn. Of all the ghosts that have been reported at the inn, the most regularly seen is the ghost of a man in a tri-corn hat. It is stated that in the early nineteenth century a man was standing at what is now 'Mary Yellan's bar',

named after Daphne du Maurier's character. Whilst drinking a tankard of ale alone at the bar he was summoned outside. He calmly placed his half-drunk ale down and disappeared into the dark night, never to return. The following morning his lifeless body was discovered on the moor. The verdict for his death was murder, yet the perpetrator was never caught. His ghost is often seen in the bar area and sitting on the wall outside the inn.

On some nights the sounds of hooves can be heard clip-clapping over the cobbled stones outside the inn. Yet when looking through the windows, nothing is to be seen. The sight of a man on horseback has also been seen on foggy nights outside the old coaching house. The hauntings are not just outside the inn, but

Small bar at Jamaica Inn.

View of the A30 from the front of Jamaica Inn.

almost every area in the old part of the public house has had reporting's of unusual activity.

On visiting Jamaica Inn early in 2011, I was able to talk to Sean Mellor, who runs the bookshop and museum onsite. Sean has worked at the inn for four years and has said that although he has felt strange things at the inn, he has never encountered a full-blown apparition. He mentioned that a staff member, who has worked at Jamaica Inn for twelve years, has never experienced anything supernatural; however, others who have started work more recently have repeatedly acknowledged unusual activity.

The inn has four haunted bedrooms – rooms 3, 4, 5 and 6 – in which many

guests have reported experiencing some unusual activity. In one case, a lady from a big company up north was staying in one of the rooms when she awoke during the night to find that the television in the room was on. She was certain that she had turned the television off before falling sleep but, without another thought, reached for the remote control on the bed to turn it off. At that point the remote control flew off the bed and disappeared. Unable to immediately find the remote control, the lady manually turned off the television and returned to sleep. In the morning, she eventually found the remote control hidden underneath the bed – in the middle of the floor. She was bemused as to how it could have

Guests on a public Haunted Happenings evening in the notorious Room 3 at Jamaica Inn.

got there. The walls were some distance from the bed and therefore the chances of it rebounding off the walls and under the bed were slim. She replaced the remote control on the bedside table and promptly left the inn. Later that day, a cleaner was freshening up the room when she found the lady's computer flash drive underneath the bed. When the inn contacted the woman, she could not understand how this device could have possibly ended up there – the last thing she had done before leaving the room was to retrieve the remote control, and there was certainly nothing else under the bed at that time.

This is just one of the many hundreds of reports that have been left by visitors and guests at the inn since 1970, when Jamaica Inn set up a 'Ghost Visitors Book' where people can leave their comments or accounts of strange experiences after a night at the inn. The book has recently been updated to a new notebook due to the old one being full. Reading the book, it is plain to see that many people have experienced strange activity here, mainly in the bedrooms and in the bar areas. So, is Jamaica Inn one of the most haunted inns in Britain?

The Ghost Club Society, the oldest organisation in the world associated with psychical research, investigated at the inn in October 1998. Michael Williams, who was a member of the Ghost Club at that time, writes about his experiences in his

Left *The 'Ghost Visitors Book', detailing ghostly guest experiences.*

Below *An example of a few entries from the 'Ghost Visitors Book'.*

book *Ghosts around Bodmin Moor.* While sitting in the small bar with eight other members of the team, between 11 p.m. and 2 a.m. he felt a kind of 'psychic electricity'. It was fairly dark but a little light was bleeding in from the main bar. Five of the team members reported seeing what appeared to be a man sitting in a chair. Upon turning on the main light, they noticed that a container with logs was in the area they were looking at and that the man had disappeared. There were no chairs in this area and the geography of the room looked much different in the dark. They concluded that they must have experienced some sort of time-slip and may have been viewing the room as it was many years ago. What makes this account interesting is that over half of the members in the room reported seeing the same thing. Two other members were unsure and two reported seeing nothing. Multiple witness accounts help to strengthen an argument for a particular experience or event because it is unlikely that many different people will hallucinate the same thing at the same time. Michael described the man as being non-distinct, like a 'painting that had faded'. He strongly believes that the man was present in the room and that he had seen an apparition from the past. For Michael, what makes Jamaica Inn impressive is that 'a steady stream of staff and visitors have given first-hand accounts of events which defy logical explanation'.

In 2001, the Ghost Club revisited Jamaica Inn and once again the small bar produced some profound results. As before, with many members present, the team suddenly became aware of an aroma of pipe tobacco. Although smoking in public houses was still legal at this point, what makes this intriguing was that none of the team members had previously smoked or were smoking in that room at the time. More beguilingly, the smell evaporated and, later on in the evening, seemed to return, with many people noticing it. Michael saw this as confirmation of the supernatural at work.

With the inn running its own ghost-hunting evenings for the public, it is understandable then that more reports of paranormal activity have been documented. I was lucky enough to be invited along to two commercial weekends at Jamaica Inn with a professional national company called Haunted Happenings. On both occasions the event was fully booked with over thirty people attending, all with differing experiences and expectations for the evening ahead. As is often the case, the group was made up of believers, sceptics and outright non-believers. With such a mix of people, it was interesting to find out how they would get on during the evening's events. Having never attended a commercial ghost-hunting event, I was unsure as to how the company would operate, but was very pleasantly surprised to find that the investigators were both professional and realistic in presenting previous experiences at the inn. A device we use regularly on investigations is the EMF (Electro-Magnetic Fields) device,

The Haunted Happenings team with guests on one of their popular ghost nights at Jamaica Inn.

the K2 meter. Many groups favour this visually pleasing device for its flashing range of colours when EMF is present, mainly used for attempting communication with the spirit world. Unfortunately, many man-made electrical components can set off the K2 and allow false readings to be recorded. Mobile phones are an example of such a device that could falsify and bewilder the public into believing that a paranormal event is occurring. Haunted Happenings make a point of requesting that guests turn off their mobile phones during an investigation for just this reason – that they can react with certain equipment. Paul Dutton, Haunted Happenings lead investigator, is always first to debunk any K2 activity by asking if anyone has their mobile phone on or any other

disruptive electronic devices. With my worries at ease – this commercial group were indeed proficient and upstanding in their investigative techniques – I was prepared for the evening ahead.

First on the agenda was a tour of the inn. Paul split us into two large groups and took each one in turn around the venue. Along the way Paul told stories of ghostly goings-on at each location before asking the group how they were feeling and whether anything untoward had happened. A short period of time was spent listening and watching quietly at each point, to see if any contact could be made with the other side. At the end of the tour the teams were swapped around and while the second team went on the tour, the first team got to learn about the

Paul Dutton from Haunted Happenings leads a group in a vigil in the museum.

The ghost hunters gather in the old stables, eagerly waiting for something to happen.

equipment and ghost-hunting techniques in an interactive workshop. This set the members up for an evening of investigation in three separate vigils around the inn. The evening eventually concluded at 4 a.m., when people were able to leave or stay the night at this haunted location. Having graced the inn on two separate occasions with Haunted Happenings, I was interested to see if there was any correlation in collated evidence from the sixty or so people that had attended across the two events. Remarkably enough, I was surprised to find that certain members of the public had indeed shared similar experiences in particular locations across the two evenings. Baring in mind that the evenings were over a month apart, and only one member of the public attended both events, it was astounding to see that at least three experiences matched perfectly in the same location on the two distinct nights. The first, a strong emotional experience, was felt in bedroom 3, the biggest of all the bedrooms. On the first investigation, a lady called Kara sat on the windowsill in this room. Within minutes she began crying inconsolably and was forced to leave the room. When interviewed, she said that she felt as though she had lost someone very close, someone she loved very much. Interestingly, on the second investigation, another woman, who also sat on the windowsill, began crying and shaking and had to be taken out of the room. She too claimed to feel as though she had lost a loved one, but after leaving the room she felt fine again. It wasn't until the second investigation that we discovered that this strong emotional feeling was related to the history between rooms 5, 4 and 3. It has been reported that the ghost of a woman carrying a baby has been seen wandering through the wall from room 5, through room 4 and finally into room 3. It is thought that the baby was stillborn or had died a little after birth. Such a loss would certainly coincide with the feelings that the two women experienced while sitting on the windowsill.

The second correlation was found in the museum, where a tall black shadow is known to dominate the area near the fire exit, at the furthest side near the road. On the first investigation, a man reported seeing a tall, black figure standing 'in his face', near the same area. Feeling uncomfortable, he moved slightly to the left in order to adjust his eyes, assuming it was a trick of light, but the figure moved with him. After a while he said that it had 'become lighter' all of a sudden and that the 'black mass' had gone. On the second investigation, a lady stood exactly where the gentleman had stood and also reported seeing a 'tall dark figure' standing in front of her. Believing it was another member of the team, she reached out to touch them only to find nothing there. Immediately she became hysterical and was forced to leave the area, shaking uncontrollably. When interviewed, she said that she felt very 'intimidated' by this figure and that he seemed to be 'right in her face'. She promptly retired to the

An intrepid member of the public attempts to coax a child spirit to move the ball balanced precariously on her hand.

bar area, saying that she did not 'want to return to the museum ever again'. Although this area is known for this frightening event, it was a great pleasure for me to attend two different evenings and find a direct correlation between statements from two different people. Even a long-standing member of staff, Julia, who does an exceptional job catering for the many guests and investigators, has declared that she would not enter the museum on her own.

Finally, the third direct correlation is probably the most reported of all. Paul described how a member of the public had previously taken a photo of a glass cabinet with an elephant inside, in the museum. The gentleman took three photos in quick succession, however, in the second photo there was a clear image of a child's face glaring back through the glass cabinet. This photo can be seen on the Haunted Happenings website (www. hauntedhappenings.co.uk). It is widely known that children have been seen and sensed in the museum, and a number of guests have reported feeling their clothes being tugged at waist level, their hands being touched or held, and the feeling of something brushing past their legs. Three or four people reported this feeling on the first night I tagged along with Haunted Happenings, and concurrently another three or four also described this experience when I attended on the second night. With so many experiences and so much history at the inn, it is no surprise that these events are so popular and frequently sell out. Many of the guests that attended both nights said they would quite happily return for another evening of investigation. Although my personal experiences at the inn have to date been limited, I am sure to return to the inn in the near future in search of ghosts!

The following experiences are the most reported phenomena at the inn: mysterious footsteps heard walking on floorboards above, the sound of horses hooves on gravel/cobbled stone, wardrobe doors opening, electrical goods turning on and off, batteries draining abnormally during paranormal investigations, the feeling of being touched or breathed on, the feeling of being watched, dark shadows appearing and moving around the bar, the tri-corn hat man sitting on a wall outside, an American airman (whose body was recovered from the moor after crashing and removed to the inn), and, in bedroom 5, guests have reported seeing a woman in eighteenth-century clothing standing over the bed. There are probably many, many more tales to tell from Jamaica Inn.

Is Jamaica Inn one of the most haunted hostelries in Britain? It certainly seems to have all the ingredients, and whether it is or not it definitely appears to be a very active location! It is undoubtedly worth visiting for an ale and some good food, but, if you are feeling brave enough, why not book into one of the four haunted bedrooms and spend an evening with Haunted Happenings on one of their popular ghost nights.

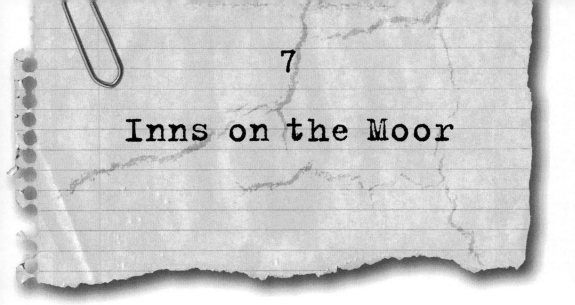

7

Inns on the Moor

BODMIN Moor is host to many pubs, inns and taverns which are dotted across the vast rugged landscape. Many of these public houses date back hundreds of years and would have played host to the travellers who regularly trekked the moorland from Cornwall to Devon. Others would have accommodated the likes of highwaymen, who scoured the main routes across the moor for likely travellers and robbed them of any wealth they may have. The inns would have been a great place to find appropriate marks, and they would watch and wait until the traveller became a vulnerable target. Jamaica Inn was renowned for smugglers and wreckers and the immense stories of ghostly encounters experienced at this inn can be read in chapter six. However, this chapter is devoted specifically to some of the other historic, and haunted, inns to be found on Bodmin Moor.

The Market Inn, St Cleer

The first pub in this chapter is located in the village of St Cleer. As a child I grew up in this village, just around the corner from the Market Inn. My parents would frequent this local and I remember visiting this hub of the community on many occasions. It is one of two pubs found in the village, the other, The Stag Inn, is a more modern-looking building, which has changed hands a number of times over the last five years and is not included here as no paranormal activity has been reported. The stone-built Market Inn sits next to the thirteenth-century church and, although it looks older than The Stag Inn, it is the newer of the two pubs. The inn has had an unhappy past. In 2005, the then pub manager, Christopher Adams, had his whole life ahead of him with his beautiful partner and eighteen-month old daughter. One morning, he rose to feed his daughter before waking his partner.

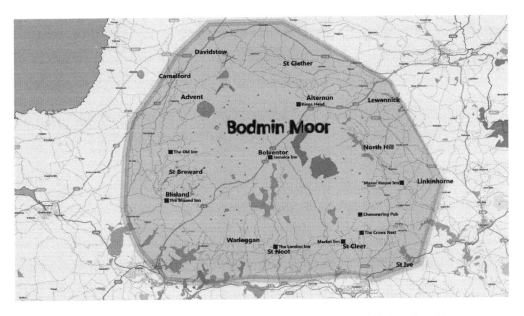

Map showing the location of the haunted inns and pubs on Bodmin Moor. (Map © OpenStreetMap contributors, CC-BY-SA. www.openstreetmap.org)

During the course of the morning the couple fell out and a full blown argument ensued. In a fit of rage Mr Adams reached for a nearby cricket bat and bludgeoned his partner and daughter to death. Although the events did not happen on the inn's premises, the argument was allegedly about his working hours and time spent in the bar at the inn. Incidentally, Mr Adams was sentenced to a minimum of twenty years in prison.

The pub itself was built in 1860 and was managed by landlady Elizabeth Lord for the first forty-three years until 1903. Coincidently, she is buried in the church grounds opposite the Market Inn. Up until 1860 there were only two pubs in the village; these were The Sportsman pub, which became the old police house, and The Stag Inn. The Market Inn was

originally built to become a miner's hotel for the new up-and-coming industry just a few miles up the road at Minions. They planned to cater for the hundreds of men who would want a refreshing beer after a long day in the mines. The Stag, whose customers were predominantly farmers, were not happy with the new pub or the new cliental that graced it. This was most likely to do with the fact that the miners had stripped some of the farmers' land, and obviously the farmers would not have been happy with that arrangement. It was said that you belonged to either one pub or the other, visiting both was heavily frowned upon and you were seen as a traitor for stepping over the threshold of the competitors' inn. This tradition continued through the ages and was continued even up until five years ago.

The Market Inn is currently managed by Paul and Penny O'Brien, who, at the time of writing, had been pouring pints at the inn for over five years. When I spoke to Penny, it was evident that she had experienced quite a bit of ghostly activity at the premises, although she seemed very calm and nonchalant about it. 'If I leave them alone, they leave me alone,' she said, smiling. One of Penny's friends is known to have psychic tendencies and she has visited the inn on a number of occasions in the last five years. Penny told me that the spirit of Elizabeth Lord has been seen and felt wandering the corridors and living quarters upstairs. When Penny's friend enters the pub, she develops a headache due to the number of spirits that reside at the inn. Only a handful of these are long-term occupants, while most seem to come in visitation. This is true for the majority of pubs, where it is not unusual to meet a long-gone local sitting observantly at the end of the bar. Sometimes, this is indicated by the strong smell of tobacco or pipe smoke, more noticeable since the smoking ban was introduced in 2007. Another former landlady, believed to be Mother Payne Muriel, is known to roam the bar area of the inn.

The previous landlady used to wake to find broken glasses behind the bar, when the night before they were shelved safely. The spirit of Mother Payne Muriel has been blamed for this activity. She may also be responsible for moving items in the kitchen, as well as throwing bowls and

The Market Inn at St Cleer.

The lounge area of the Market Inn, which was the original bar.

dishes on the floor. Penny tells me that on a visit by an Environmental Health Officer, the officer was struck on the back of the head by a metal bowl in the kitchen. When she glanced round to see who had thrown it, no one was there. Apparently, this particular officer now undertakes visits from the bar area only. Although primarily blamed on Mother Payne Muriel, there is apparently a gentleman ghost that resides in the cellar area called 'Sam'. He is a very playful spirit and likes to play tricks on people as well as pinch their bum. On more than one occasion 'Sam' has pinched the bums of two women and, with such a playful nature, may be to blame for the kitchen poltergeist–like activity.

Penny's psychic friend was out for the evening and returned to change her shoes. She was used to being in the pub upstairs alone and often stayed the weekend, however, on this occasion, as she was tying her shoelaces, she noticed something out of the corner of her eye. She raised her head slowly and saw, standing in front of her, a full blown apparition of what she described as a 'miner carrying his helmet under his arm'. Such was her surprise that she fled the pub into the night and vowed never to stay there again (although I have been told that she still frequents the bar!). Penny informed me that most activity seems to occur when the pub changes hands. Many different landladies have tried their luck at running The Market Inn, but only a few seem to stay for any length of time. Penny is one of the longer tenants – having been at the pub for five years – but one thing seems to be common among all new residents, and that is the heightened levels of physical activity experienced. It is as though the spirits don't like change and when they are forced to endure new management, they kick off and show their disapproval. Within the first few months of Penny running the pub, phenomena such as broken glass behind the bar, beer pouring wrong, various kitchen items being found on the floor and problems with light bulbs blowing became common. After a few months this activity seemed to dissipate and things got back to normal.

I asked Penny about any unusual paranormal activity experienced by guests or locals at the inn. She said that under a previous landlady, a man once rented the bottom bedroom. The landlady happened to pop out for a few hours and, when she returned, she decided to make sure the gentleman was comfortable and see if he needed anything. Upon knocking she received no answer and so opened the door and let herself in. The room was empty apart from a few items of the man's clothing on the bed. Assuming he had popped out, the landlady went back downstairs to run the pub. Hours later, when the gentleman had still not returned, she began to worry. No one knows what had happened to this gentleman but he never returned to collect the last of his items. This is the same room that Penny's friend saw the miner with his helmet under his arm.

Another entity resides in the private living room upstairs. Penny's psychic friend has mentioned that there is a strict, abrupt and unhappy man called 'Samuel' who seems to be looking for something. She states that he does not like disorder or untidiness, and she feels that he is looking for an accounts ledger, probably for the pub. Although Penny is aware of his spirit and the others that haunt The Market Inn, she says that they all live together with mutual respect for each other. While she has let her friend 'investigate' the many spirits of the inn, she has never had a paranormal group at the pub. I asked her if she would consider a proper investigation and she replied with a fairly uncompromising 'no'. As mentioned before, Penny believes that if she leaves them alone then they won't cause her any trouble. The Market Inn has its fair share of ghosts but it is nice to see that the landlady does not want to exploit this side of the pub in St Cleer.

The Crows Nest, near Darite

Situated between Commonmoor and Darite is a sixteenth-century stone-walled inn called The Crows Nest. It is a charming, low-ceiling pub and restaurant with a warm, inviting atmosphere, especially in the winter months with the trance-inducing wood-burning fire at one end of the bar. The building started out as a miner's captain cottage, but other reports claim that it was also a brothel at some point. Either way, The Crows Nest is a fantastic location. The inside is decorated with old photographs from the area, lanterns, and the ceiling is lined with horse stirrups and bits. One end of the pub sports the fabulous raging fire, while down the other side a recess seating area can be found. With such a warm atmosphere it is hard to imagine that such a location could be home to many different spirits of the non-alcoholic kind.

Traditionally, four different ghosts have been associated with the inn. The first is a heartbroken bride waiting for her love to return from working in the mine — which he never does. The second is an elderly lady who regularly returns to the Crows Nest for a late night tipple, probably a local lass who once revered the walls of the old pub. The third is an old gentleman who has been seen walking straight through the bar wall to the outside area of the building. Finally, footsteps are often heard upstairs when there is no one up there at all. Michael Williams, author of *Ghosts around Bodmin Moor* and a writer for the *Cornish Guardian*, was fortunate enough to visit and investigate The Crows Nest in 2003. He was joined by Joan Bettison, a local lady who is well known for her ability to heal animals and people; she is also a fond investigator of the paranormal. During their visit they used crystals and mediumship to see if they could contact any of the spirits that wandered the inn. One of the first spirits they managed to contact was a young boy, who apparently came to the pub to

collect his wages after working down the mine. Interestingly, the boy had come in visitation and was not related to the pub itself. The medium was informed that he was aware of the Charlotte Dymond murder of 1844 (*see* chapter three). Poor Charlotte was murdered near Rough Tor, about 15 miles from The Crows Nest. Due to the public interest in the case at the time, the boy would probably have known about her untimely death from community gossip and news, as opposed to being in the vicinity at the time, but it would have been interesting to know for sure how he knew about the killing. The medium also picked up that this boy was tragically killed in an accident in the mine when he was just fifteen.

Abigail and Tim have been running The Crows Nest for the last eleven years. One of the most interesting experiences was when Abigail was cashing up the till late one night and she noticed what seemed to be a swirl of smoke circulating below a light near the entrance to the bar. Upon closer inspection, she noticed that the smoke appeared to contain tiny grains of sand. The smoke did not appear anywhere else in the pub and had never been seen before. Abigail entered the kitchen to get Tim to come and observe it for himself, however, on returning, the 'smoke' was gone. A few days later, Abigail noticed the same swirling smoke again and called for Tim; this time, he also witnessed the bizarre phenomena in the bar. It was considered that the smoke was the product of the open fire in the

The Crows Nest.

A photo showing the bar area of the Crows Nest with the many horse stirrups and bits hanging from the low ceiling.

The Cornish Guardian published an article on Michael Williams' investigation at The Crows Nest in 2003.

pub, however, after managing the pub for eleven years and having an open fire often burning, especially in the winter months, it would be prudent to assume that such an event would be witnessed on more than two occasions. Swirling smoke with glistening elements is well known in the paranormal world as potentially being the attempted manifestation of an entity. It is believed that a spirit is endeavouring to use the energy around it to 'visualise' itself, but, due to a lack of energy, may only manage to conjure a wispy white mist. After discussing this event with one of their customers, that person subsequently brought in a photo showing a similar incident in their grandmother's house.

Tim informed me of the time he found a row of broken glasses behind the bar. What makes this more intriguing was that the row of broken pint glasses were found at the back of the glass shelf. On inspection, it appeared as if the glasses had fallen over and then smashed, forcing the following rows of glasses forward. It is hard to see how a row of pint glasses, trapped by other pint glasses, could fall forward and consequently smash. Tim told me that he often has the feeling of being watched when the pub is empty. Abigail has been in the cellar of the pub, changing the barrels or tidying the stock, and has felt as though there was someone else there; she has also had the same feeling upstairs. So, are these experiences only witnessed by paranormal investigators and the managers? It seems not. Tony Symonds from Hurlers Halt, in Minions, explained the following to Michael Williams, who ran it in a article for the *Cornish Guardian* in 2003:

> It happened in 1999. I saw this woman in the style of the mid-1800s. She was medium height and had grey hair. It was about 10.30 in the evening and there were, I think, eight people present. They saw nothing, but I saw this figure in the dining room and she walked out through the window. Apparently in the past the window had been a doorway.

Other locals have reported seeing a boy wandering through the pub and also a 'dark shadow' in the doorway when nobody was near the door. Mrs Crowe, who used to run the pub many moons ago, has testified to hearing phantom footsteps on the old spiral staircase, which now leads to the cottage next door.

With so much history surrounding the old building, it is understandable that people will experience certain levels of supernatural activity. Thick granite walls are theoretically known to store events in history – this is recognised in the paranormal world as 'stone-tape' theory. One thing is for sure – the pub has a relaxing and inviting atmosphere and it is obvious that any ghosts that still reside or visit this amazing inn are friendly and auspicious and in no way mean any harm. If you find yourself travelling around Bodmin Moor be sure to stop off at The Crows Nest and soak up the atmosphere with a nice pint of beer.

The Cheesewring, Minions

The Cheesewring pub is located in the highest village in Cornwall, Minions, which is over 300 meters above sea level. The pub manager, Marcia, who has ran the bar/hotel for over thirteen years, had many stories to tell me. Being a local lady, she was full of useful information and history from the area. It is believed the Cheesewring pub was built in the 1870s, although an interesting titbit of information suggests that the building may have been moved from nearby Henwood, where a similar structure was once found. This pub would have been used by the miners in the area after finishing a long day's graft at the nearby Phoenix mines on the moor itself. The mines, now defunct and dilapidated, still scatter the rugged moorland just yards from the warm atmosphere of the pub.

Phoenix Mine in the early 1900s. (Photo courtesy of The Cheesewring pub)

This leads us into one of the most well-known ghosts seen here, that of a woman. Upstairs in the hotel is located a double bedroom, available for guests. In a similar manner to The Crows Nest (see above), it has been reported by both staff and guests alike that a ghostly woman has been seen staring out of the window, looking disconsolately towards the moorland. It is believed that she is waiting for her husband to return from a day's work down the mines; however, as is often found with these tales, he was never to return. Unfortunately, he was probably one of the many people killed in the mines in the latter part of the nineteenth century. The pub was recently visited by a psychic who picked up on this lady. He mentioned that her name was Maggie Tresillian, and that she had committed suicide after losing her 'one true love'. It

is thought that she still resides at the pub, eagerly awaiting her lover's return from the mines. As well as this sad spectre, the inn is also known for its more mischievous residents.

The double bedroom plays host to other ghosts of a more spirited nature. One particular ghost likes to wind up the room's residents by waiting for them to leave the room and then promptly locks them out. The residents have returned to their room to find the door locked with the key still inside. When they manage to gain entry to the room, the key would be where they had left it. In addition to this, a staff member returned one evening to hear music playing in the room and the door locked, once again, from the inside. When she managed to gain access to the room she found that the radio in the corner was on and it was playing popular music, although it was clearly off when she left. Marcia told me that her dog was also aggrieved by the offending room and would not go near it. Often he would stop, glare and growl at the room when passing, before running off in the direction he was going.

It is not just the upstairs that hosts rascally spirits. Located downstairs in the lounge area of the pub is a fairly heavy brass pineapple ornament. The embellishment itself splits into two pieces, a lid, and a container part for storing small items, such as buttons or money. One particular day, when the pub was quite busy, the pineapple brass lid ejected itself off the ornament and promptly hit a patron in the back of the leg, luckily without causing any harm, although the patron was a little bruised. When the gentleman turned around to face the culprit no one was standing near the ornament. Various people admitted seeing the pineapple lid launch itself from the side and hitting the gentleman's leg. Apparently, the lid has been seen flying off its base and into the middle of the floor on many occasions.

One Sunday lunchtime, the present landlord of the pub, Gary Stone, was eating a meal with his wife in the lounge area. Pub manager Marcia had just mopped the floor leading through the bar to the kitchen and was keen to keep it clean. She enlisted the help of Gary's four-year-old son to keep an eye out and make sure no one stepped over the threshold. A short time later a little voice asked Marcia, 'Who is that man?'

'What man?' Marcia replied.

'The man that just walked past here and through that wall,' the boy announced. He then reported seeing the man 'walk back

The Cheesewring pub on a particularly misty winter's day.

The brass pineapple base and lid, which has been seen 'thrown' at people from its stationary position.

Eventually, the dilapidated structure was knocked down and a new building was constructed in 1900. During the three years it took to build the new inn, patrons were able to use the little chapel across the way to receive their daily intake of alcohol. It was said that chaplains and councillors became concerned with this prospect as it seems they were selling too much ale. In 1903, the building was finished and renamed the Royal Oak Hotel, before being converted back to a picturesque inn around the mid-1990s and being named The Blisland Inn once again.

According to a previous landlady of the inn, when it was the Royal Oak Hotel it is believed that back in the 1920s, a resident at the hotel, in a state of depression and misery, committed suicide by hanging himself from the rafters.

When I had the pleasure of visiting the location with my mother I was immediately taken aback by the cosy and inviting bar – it was not hard to see why this inn won CAMRA's National Pub of the Year in 2001. We were greeted by Lorraine, a lovely barmaid, who welcomed us to the inn and had various tales to tell. A few locals were relaxing and reading in the bar when I made my purpose known; that I was a ghost hunter looking for any ghost-related information concerning The Blisland Inn. The response I received was mixed and I soon became aware that I was surrounded by people who may not agree with such subject matter; however, it was not long before both my

through the wall'. It would seem that, possibly in the early twentieth century, there would have been a door leading to a cellar area where the boy had seen the man. Had Gary's son seen his first ghost? This pub is definitely on the books for an investigation soon!

The Blisland Inn, Blisland

Situated in the village of Blisland, deep in the heart of Bodmin Moor, is The Blisland Inn. Originally built in the seventeenth century, this thatched ale-house was the hub of the community.

mother, who is a devout Christian, and I were being regaled with a story about the 'Death Chair' (Dead Man's Chair), which sits prominently near the bar. When we asked, 'Why is it called the Death Chair?' we were told that, apparently, when the chair was situated on the other side of the bar, near the fireplace, over a period of time a number of people chose to sit in the offending chair. Over time those people died one by one. Superstition soon took over and people started to avoid sitting in the chair with a passion. Indeed, no one now sits in the 'Death Chair'. Unfortunately, it seems that this is as far as ghostly goings-on at the inn appear to go. Although the ceiling is laden with hanging mugs and the walls dressed in all types of different barometers, Gary Marshall,

the landlord of sixteen years, and his staff claim they have not felt, sensed or seen any unusual activity at this pub. It just goes to show that not all old, quaint and isolated moorland pubs are haunted!

The Old Inn, St Breward

The Old Inn at St Breward is believed to have been built in the eleventh century, specifically to house the monks who built the church. Darren Wills has been the landlord of the Old Inn since 1999 and his partner, Richard, has lived at the old building for over six years. I asked them if they had experienced any paranormal activity while living and working at the inn. This was their reply:

The Blisland Inn today.

Our most frequent experience which has been heard by most of the locals is someone walking across the main bar ceiling even though no one is upstairs, most of the staff including myself have heard this. Margaret our long serving cleaner has seen all sorts of things, before the restaurants new bar was open she had seen a folder move horizontally in mid-air before it promptly fell straight down onto the floor. She has also seen a set of footprints walking straight into the wall from our main bar into the middle bar (the original part of the building) after mopping the floor.

Richard has also seen a cat walking through the restaurant part of the pub. Although the pub does have its own resident cat, at this time it was asleep in the main bar. When Richard turned around to look again, the cat had mysteriously vanished. The previous owners of the inn were also aware of a strange atmosphere, mostly felt in the spare bedroom upstairs. For Richard it has the strangest feeling – more than any other room in the pub. He says that he has slept in the spare room on a number of occasions and has noticed a significant drop in temperature, as well as it being unusually quiet. Considering this room is located over the pub's main fire in the bar, the temperature should not have been a problem.

Richard informs me that on one occasion Darren's father, while looking after the pub for Darren and Richard when they were on holiday, was awoken one night by someone – or something – running its hand down his back. The feeling brought chills to his spine! Part of the pub built in the early 1980s had chalk boards on a wall, advertising the menu's 'specials'. Before 2006, the manager used to write offers and special meal deals on this board regularly. On several occasions, after completing it, the following day a part of the board would be rubbed out. At first the manager thought one of the staff members had a grudge against him, however, after interviewing the staff he was unable to explain it.

Finally, Richard told me of an ongoing supernatural occurrence. Every evening the tables in the restaurant are stripped and wiped down ready for the following day. Nevertheless, upon waking the following morning, they regularly find salt scattered on some of the tables which have obviously not been used overnight.

Other Bodmin Moor pub ghosts

The King's Head at Altarnun is said to be visited by one of its former landladies, Peggy Bray. Lately, a paranormal investigation group attended the fifteenth-century coaching inn to see what they could find. Although reports seem to suggest the evening may have been a fairly quiet one, the group did pick up an interesting audio anomaly. As reported in the *Cornish Guardian* on 16 November 2011: 'The team had gone to bed around

3 a.m. but the tape recorder at 3.20 picked up the sound of heavy footsteps moving across the carpeted floor of bedroom number 3, an unoccupied double bedroom with a haunted reputation'. They also reported hearing a strange clicking noise likened to an old-fashioned door latch being lifted off its catch. Other reports suggest a particular visitor who, when staying for the night, repeatedly heard tapping on her window. On investigating the noise, she was astounded to find no one there. Recent experiences include the landlady's private quarters' door being locked when she had deliberately left it unlocked, and the oven in the private kitchen upstairs mysteriously turning itself on.

The Manor House Inn at Rilla Mill, near Callington, is known to be the home of phantom footsteps heard coming from upstairs, where the sounds are apparently always traced back to an empty bedroom. Although the current landlady has not experienced any unusual activity in her six-year-tenancy to date, customers and staff have. One such staff member was working behind the bar one afternoon when she noticed the black silhouette of a man standing at the far side of the bar. When she moved closer to identify him, he disappeared without a trace. The same shadowy figure has also been seen by more than one customer, and some people have reported feeling uneasy and anxious when entering the premises, although it should be mentioned that this has nothing to do with the pub, the staff or the customers themselves, who offer a very welcoming atmosphere at all times. I was informed by

The front of the King's Head at Five Lanes, near Altarnun.

The Manor House at Rilla Mill.

a local lady that she was aware of a brutal murder which took place in a barn by the pub. She had heard that a man was killed after he was found dancing with another man's partner, could this be the shadowy man that people have seen?

There are many more olde-worlde pubs and inns scattered across Bodmin Moor, many with their own stories and legends to tell; unfortunately, I am unable to recount all the tales here! If you find yourself straddling the eerie common between Bodmin and Launceston, then why not visit the local inn for an ale and a bite to eat and ask the bar person about their own tale of the unexpected!

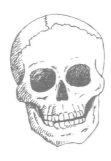

Afterword

DURING the research for this book I have experienced many adventures and much excitement. I have been exposed to all weather and found myself knee-high in mud, marsh and various other natural substances I would rather forget. From the tops of tors to the hidden valleys in the moors, I have been welcomed at all times by the communities that reside across this desolate landscape. At times I felt a little uncomfortable entering the various pubs and inns, many of which housed a few locals who were obviously puzzled at my demeanour; dressed oddly in shorts (as I always am, regardless of the month), carrying a camera, a tripod and a trusty notepad. I would regularly approach the bar towards the equally puzzled-looking bar steward, surrounded by an air of silence, before I would ask an equally puzzling question: 'Please can you tell me if you have ever experienced any unusual activity?' A frown would pass over their

A broken log litters the path around Caradon Hill.

faces before a question was thrust back at me, 'What kind of unusual activity?' At this point I knew I was in for an interesting period as I tried to explain who I was and what I was doing – without attempting to sound like a delirious man who has just wandered off the moors after being lost for months on end. Thankfully, I was warmly accepted and intrigued by the stories which began to flow.

Although a lot of historical information has been referenced and used in this book from other material, much information has been quoted from or experienced by those who live locally on the moor. Along this unforgettable journey I have been honoured to meet countless people who have graced me with their knowledge and provided me with facts that I would have struggled to come across without their assistance. An example of this was during the writing of Chapter Six. I wanted to include a photo of Daphne du Maurier and, when applying to use this photo, I was privileged to be contacted by Daphne's son, Kits Browning, who has provided me with information as well as sending me a fabulous signed copy of *Vanishing Cornwall* by Daphne and himself, which I would recommend wholeheartedly to anyone who has an interest in Cornwall.

It is fair to say that I have only just scratched the surface of Bodmin Moor's mysteries; however, I hope that I have managed to enlighten and entertain you, because if I haven't, then I haven't achieved my goal.

Select Bibliography and Further Reading

Books

Andrews, Stuart & Higgs, Jason, *Paranormal Cornwall* (The History Press, 2010)

Axford, E.C., *The Cornish Moor: A Brief Study of Bodmin Moor* (Snell & Cowling, Date unknown)

Bishop, Ray, *North Cornwall Camera* (Bossiney Books, 1994)

du Maurier, Daphne, *Vanishing Cornwall* (Virago Press, 2007)

Henry Harris, J. & Raven-Hill, L., *Cornish Saints and Sinners*, (John Lane, The Bodley Head, 1906)

Johnson, Bill, *The History of Bodmin Jail*, (Bodmin Town Museum, 2006)

Langdon, A., *Stone Crosses in East Cornwall*, (Federation of Old Cornwall Societies, 2005)

Langdon, A.G., *Old Cornish Crosses*, (Cornwall Books, 1896)

Mullins, Rose, *The Inn on the Moor: A History of Jamaica Inn* (PR Publishing, 2009)

Munn, Pat, *The Charlotte Dymond Murder* (Bodmin Books, 1978)

Munn, Pat, *The Story of Cornwall's Bodmin Moor* (Bodmin Books, 2009)

Newman, Paul, *Haunted Cornwall* (Tempus Publishing, 2005)

Straffon, Cheryl, *The Earth Mysteries Guide to Bodmin Moor and North Cornwall* (Meyn Mamvro Publications, 1993)

Tennyson, Alfred Lord, *The Passing of Arthur: Idylls of The King (1809-1892)*

Thompson, E.V., *100 years on Bodmin Moor* (Bossiney Books, 1984)

Underwood, Peter, *Ghosts of Cornwall* (Bossiney Books, 1998) Westwood, Jennifer, *A Guide to Legendary Britain* (Grafton Books, 1985)

White, Paul, *King Arthur's Footsteps* (Bossiney Books, 2008)

White, Paul, *Ancient Cornwall* (Bossiney Books, 2008)

Williams, Michael, *Supernatural Search in Cornwall* (Bossiney Books, 1991)

Williams, Michael, *Ghosts around Bodmin Moor* (Bossiney Books, 2005)

Websites

www.haunted-britain.com

www.mysteriousbritain.co.uk

www.myweb.tiscali.co.uk

www.themodernantiquarian.com

www.bodminmoor.co.uk

www.historynet.com

www.jamaicainn.co.uk

www.pandiawarleggan.com

www.thisisnorthcornwall.com

www.bodminjail.org

www.westcountryviews.co.uk

www.soulsearcherskernow.com

www.hauntedhappenings.co.uk

www.heritageaction.wordpress.com

www.thisiscornwall.co.uk

www.67notout.com

www.strangeuk.com

www.davidstowmemorialmuseum.co.uk

www.archiver.rootsweb.ancestry.com

www.stone-circles.org.uk

www.britannia.com

www.cornwalls.co.uk

www.thisisnorthcornwall.com

www.greatbritishghosttour.co.uk

www.visitoruk.com

www.connexions.co.uk

www.stevecolgan.com

www.stneot.org.uk

www.carnglaze.com

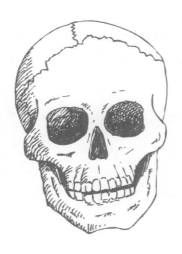

If you enjoyed this book, you may also be interested in…

Paranormal Cornwall
STUART ANDREWS & JASON HIGGS

The county of Cornwall, rich in folklore and legends, is also home to an array of paranormal activity. Drawing on historical and contemporary sources, this selection includes sightings of UFOs and big cats, ghosts, sea monsters, piskies and many other bizarre phenomena in the county. Accompanied by eyewitness interviews, press reports and previously unpublished investigation accounts carried out by the authors, *Paranormal Cornwall* is sure to appeal to everyone interested in the mysteries of the paranormal.

978 0 7524 5261 6

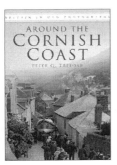

Around the Cornish Coast
PETER Q. TRELOAR

From Morwenstown in the north to Torpoint in the south, this pictorial Cornish tour traces the history of the coastal towns it encompasses, the evolution of the fishing and shipping industries and that of the railways which put these beautiful towns on the tourist route. This book will appeal to maritime enthusiasts and all those who wish to know more about the history of the coastal settlements. It is sure to evoke nostalgic memories for those who remember Cornwall over many years, whilst giving insight into the past for those visiting the area.

978 0 7524 5784 0

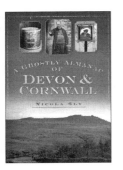

A Ghostly Almanac of Devon & Cornwall
NICOLA SLY

Contained within the pages of this book are strange tales of restless spirits appearing in streets, buildings and churchyards across the Westcountry, including a haunted German U-Boat wrecked off Padstow during the First World War, the 'Grey Lady' at the Royal Devon and Exeter Hospital, the ghost of a Dartmoor Prison inmate, a shade with a penchant for horror films at Plymouth's Reel Cinema, and the infamous 'Hairy Hands of Dartmoor', which forces drivers off the road. Richly illustrated, this chilling collection of stories will appeal to everyone interested in the South West's haunted heritage.

978 0 7524 5268 5

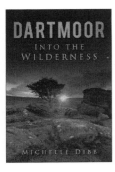

Dartmoor: Into the Wilderness
MICHELLE DIBB

From its curious stone circles and rows to its hard rocky tors, from its rich, moss-covered ancient woodlands and rushing rivers to its sparse high moor land and bleak prison, Dartmoor has inspired artists, poets and musicians for centuries. This book contains a fascinating mixture of informative facts and mysterious tales. Here you will discover the wildlife, the history, the geography, the legends, the industry, the harshness and the inspiring wonder of one of England's most popular National Parks.

978 0 7524 5929 5

Visit our website and discover thousands of other History Press books.

www.thehistorypress.co.uk